UNIVERSAL BASIC INCOME

ENDING OPPRESSIVE ECONOMICS AND BUILDING A SOCIETY

DAN PAUL

CONTENTS

INTRODUCTION

What is Universal Basic Income?

Universal Basic Income (UBI) is a policy idea that has been debated for centuries but has gained renewed attention in recent years. At its core, UBI is a simple concept: every citizen receives a regular, unconditional cash payment from the government, regardless of employment status, wealth, or any other factors. The idea is to provide a financial foundation that ensures basic needs are met, giving people the freedom to pursue education, entrepreneurship, caregiving, or any other path without the immediate pressure of economic survival.

Unlike welfare programs that require recipients to meet certain conditions—such as proving unemployment or demonstrating need—UBI is universal and unconditional. The payments are meant to supplement, rather than replace, earned income, providing financial stability in an era of rapid technological change, precarious work, and widening economic inequality.

The questions surrounding UBI are as compelling as they are complex. Would such a policy encourage creativity and economic growth, or would it discourage people from working? Can it be financially sustainable, or would it overburden taxpayers? Is it a necessary response to automation and inequality, or an unrealistic dream that ignores the realities of economic constraints?

Why This Book?

Universal Basic Income is not just a theoretical discussion—it is an idea that has been tested in pilot programs around the world, from Finland to Kenya, from Canada to the United States. As automation threatens to replace millions of jobs and economic inequality continues to rise, the conversation about UBI is becoming more urgent. Policymakers, business leaders, economists, and everyday citizens are increasingly asking: Should we implement UBI, and if so, how?

This book seeks to cut through the myths and misunderstandings about UBI. It will examine its potential benefits and drawbacks, explore how it could be funded, and analyze whether it is a viable solution to the economic challenges of the future. It will also address the political and social hurdles that stand in the way of its adoption.

By exploring both the arguments for and against UBI, this book provides a comprehensive look at one of the most debated policy ideas of our time. Whether you are a supporter, a skeptic, or someone just beginning to learn about UBI, this book will equip you with the knowledge to engage in meaningful discussions about its implications.

The Debate: Utopian Dream or Necessary Reform?

Critics of UBI argue that it is an expensive, unrealistic proposal that would disincentivize work and lead to economic stagnation. They believe that giving people "free money" will create dependency, encourage laziness, and burden the economy with unsustainable costs. Others claim that UBI is unnecessary, as existing welfare systems can be reformed to better serve those in need without a sweeping, universal program.

Supporters, on the other hand, argue that UBI is not a radical fantasy but a pragmatic solution to modern economic challenges. As automation eliminates traditional jobs and the gig economy creates instability, many believe UBI can provide a financial safety net that encourages entrepreneurship, education, and overall well-being. They see it as a way to reduce bureaucracy, eliminate poverty traps, and give individuals greater freedom over their lives.

The debate over UBI is not just an economic one—it is deeply tied to our values and beliefs about work, fairness, and the role of government in shaping society. Some see it as a moral imperative, ensuring that no one falls into destitution in an era of unprecedented technological advancement. Others view it as a misguided redistribution of wealth that undermines personal responsibility and economic efficiency.

So, is UBI a utopian dream or a necessary reform? The answer may lie somewhere in between. This book will explore both perspectives, offering a balanced analysis of what UBI is, how it could work, and what it could mean for the future of our economy and society.

No matter where you stand on the issue, one thing is clear: the conversation about Universal Basic Income is not going away. In the pages ahead, we will explore whether it is the right solution for our time—or simply an idea whose time will never come.

CHAPTER 1
A BRIEF HISTORY OF UNIVERSAL BASIC INCOME

Introduction

The idea of Universal Basic Income (UBI) may seem like a modern response to the challenges of automation and economic inequality, but its roots stretch back centuries. From early philosophical musings to real-world experiments, the concept of providing individuals with a guaranteed income has been explored in different societies under varying economic and political conditions.

In this chapter, we will examine the origins of UBI, review key pilot programs that have tested its viability, and explore how the shifting nature of work—particularly due to automation—has renewed interest in this idea.

Early Ideas of Guaranteed Income

The concept of a guaranteed income has been discussed for centuries, often in response to issues of poverty, wealth inequality, and economic instability. While not always referred to as UBI, early thinkers envisioned policies that shared similar principles.

One of the earliest recorded ideas of a basic income can be traced to the 16th century. In 1516, Sir Thomas More's *Utopia* described a society in which all individuals were provided with material security, reducing the need for crime and economic desperation. A few decades later, Spanish humanist Juan Luis Vives proposed a system of public assistance that would provide for the poor, arguing that poverty was not necessarily a moral failing but rather a structural issue.

In the 18th century, thinkers such as Thomas Paine and Marquis de Condorcet put forth more concrete proposals. Paine, one of the Founding Fathers of the United States, suggested in *Agrarian Justice* (1797) that a universal payment should be given to all citizens, funded by land taxation, as compensation for the unequal distribution of natural resources. Condorcet, a French Enlightenment philosopher, envisioned a state-driven system to provide economic security to all individuals, arguing that technological progress should benefit everyone, not just the wealthy elite.

By the 20th century, economists and policymakers began considering guaranteed income as a serious policy proposal. British economist John Maynard Keynes famously predicted in 1930 that technological advancements would lead to a future in which work was largely optional, allowing people to enjoy more leisure. While his vision of a 15-hour workweek has not materialized, his ideas about economic redistribution laid the foundation for later discussions on UBI.

Experiments and Pilot Programs Around the World

Throughout the 20th and 21st centuries, various governments and organizations have experimented with guaranteed income models, testing their effectiveness in reducing poverty, improving health and education outcomes, and encouraging economic activity.

The U.S. and the Negative Income Tax Experiments

In the 1960s and 1970s, the United States conducted a series of Negative Income Tax (NIT) experiments under Presidents Lyndon B. Johnson and Richard Nixon. These trials took place in several states, including New Jersey, Pennsylvania, and Indiana. The goal was to determine whether providing a minimum guaranteed income—through tax credits to low-income households—would encourage or discourage work.

The results were mixed. While poverty rates declined and participants reported improved well-being, some critics pointed to slight reductions in workforce participation, particularly among secondary earners (such as mothers who chose to stay home with children). Nevertheless, the experiments demonstrated that a guaranteed income could provide stability without leading to mass unemployment.

Canada: The Mincome Experiment

In the 1970s, Canada launched the "Mincome" experiment in Manitoba, providing unconditional payments to residents in the town of Dauphin. The results showed that while some individuals worked slightly less (mainly teenagers staying in school longer and new mothers spending more time with their children), overall employment remained stable. The program led to improved health outcomes, reduced hospital visits, and increased educational attainment. However, the program was eventually discontinued due to budgetary and political shifts.

Finland's Basic Income Pilot (2017-2018)

In 2017, Finland ran a two-year experiment providing 2,000 unemployed citizens with a monthly stipend of €560, with no conditions attached. The goal was to see whether UBI could reduce bureaucracy and encourage people to seek employment. While the recipients reported lower stress levels and improved well-being, the employment effects were modest. However, many experts argue that the study's limited scope did not fully test the long-term impacts of UBI.

Kenya's Ongoing Basic Income Experiment

One of the most ambitious UBI experiments is currently underway in Kenya, where the nonprofit organization GiveDirectly has been providing direct cash payments to thousands of residents in rural villages. The program, which will run for over a decade, aims to assess the long-term effects of guaranteed income on economic activity, health, and education. Early results suggest that cash recipients are using their funds to invest in businesses, improve living conditions, and increase school attendance rates.

Other Global Trials

Several other countries, including Brazil, Spain, and the Netherlands, have conducted or are considering pilot programs to evaluate UBI's impact. While each experiment has different methodologies and goals, a common finding is that recipients generally use the payments responsibly, investing in their future rather than simply spending frivolously.

The Rise of Automation and Economic Insecurity

While guaranteed income has been debated for centuries, the modern resurgence of UBI is largely driven by the rapid pace of automation and the changing nature of work.

The Threat of Job Automation

Technological advancements, particularly in artificial intelligence (AI) and robotics, are transforming industries at an unprecedented rate. Jobs that were once secure—such as manufacturing, retail, transportation, and even white-collar professions—are increasingly being automated.

Studies suggest that millions of jobs could disappear in the coming decades. A 2017 report by McKinsey & Company estimated that up to 30% of global work activities could be automated by 2030. While new jobs will emerge, the transition may leave many workers unemployed or underemployed, struggling to find meaningful work in an increasingly automated economy.

The Rise of the Gig Economy and Job Insecurity

Even for those who remain employed, the structure of work is changing. The gig economy—characterized by short-term contracts and freelance work—has replaced many traditional, stable jobs. While this model offers flexibility, it often lacks benefits like health insurance, paid leave, and job security. As a result, economic insecurity is growing, even for those who are actively working.

UBI as a Solution?

Proponents argue that UBI could serve as a safety net in this evolving economic landscape. By providing a guaranteed income, individuals would have the flexibility to retrain for new careers, start businesses, or pursue creative and caregiving roles that traditional labor markets do not adequately support. Critics, however, worry that UBI may not address deeper structural issues in the economy and could be prohibitively expensive.

Conclusion

The idea of Universal Basic Income is not new, but the conditions of the modern world have given it renewed urgency. As history has shown, guaranteed income programs can provide economic stability and social benefits without necessarily leading to widespread workforce disengagement. However, as automation accelerates and job markets become increasingly unstable, the debate over UBI will only intensify.

In the next chapter, we will explore the details of how a universal basic income could be structured, who would qualify, and what the potential economic impacts might be. Is UBI truly a solution for the 21st century, or is it just another economic experiment that will ultimately fail?

CHAPTER 2
WHO QUALIFIES FOR UNIVERSAL BASIC INCOME?

Introduction

Universal Basic Income (UBI) is often described as an unconditional payment provided to every citizen, yet the reality of implementing such a system requires careful consideration of eligibility criteria. Would UBI be given to individuals or households? Would there be economic or residency requirements? Who, if anyone, would be excluded? While the "universal" in UBI suggests inclusivity, most real-world proposals introduce some level of qualification to balance cost, effectiveness, and fairness.

This chapter explores how eligibility for UBI might be determined, the potential consequences of different approaches, and the debates surrounding who should and should not receive payments.

Individual vs. Household Eligibility

A major question in designing a UBI system is whether payments should be distributed on an individual basis or determined at the household level. Each approach has distinct advantages and challenges.

Individual Eligibility: The Purest Form of UBI

In a truly universal system, every adult would receive a basic income regardless of their marital status, household structure, or employment situation. This approach ensures maximum simplicity, fairness, and autonomy. Since each person receives the same amount, there is no need for complex calculations based on family size or shared resources.

Advantages of individual UBI:

- **Simplicity**– No need to track household composition.
- **Autonomy** – Payments go directly to individuals rather than being controlled by a spouse or head of household.
- **Avoids marriage or cohabitation penalties**– No reduction in benefits based on household income.

However, some critics argue that distributing UBI solely on an individual basis could create inefficiencies. For example, a household of two working adults would receive double the amount of UBI compared to a single parent raising children alone, even though the latter might have greater financial needs.

Household-Based UBI: A More Cost-Conscious Approach

An alternative approach is to calculate UBI based on household composition. In this model, payments might be structured in a way that provides a reduced per-person amount for those living together, recognizing that households can share costs such as rent, utilities, and food.

Advantages of household-based UBI:

- **Cost efficiency**– Reducing payments for multi-person households could make UBI more affordable.
- **Addresses economies of scale**– Recognizes that shared living arrangements lower individual costs.

However, this model raises several concerns:

- **Increased bureaucracy**– Determining household size and composition adds complexity.
- **Potential marriage penalties** – Couples or roommates might receive lower payments, discouraging cohabitation.
- **Control issues** – In some cases, one member of the household could dominate financial decisions, limiting individual autonomy.

Ultimately, whether UBI should be structured at the individual or household level depends on balancing fairness, economic feasibility, and administrative complexity. Most UBI proposals favor individual eligibility to avoid bureaucratic inefficiencies, even if this increases costs.

Economic and Residency Requirements

Although UBI is often discussed as "universal," most proposals consider placing some conditions on eligibility based on economic status or residency.

Should UBI Be Means-Tested?

One of the most controversial questions about UBI is whether it should be given to everyone regardless of income or reserved for those below a certain economic threshold.

• **Proponents of universal payments** argue that UBI should be unconditional to avoid the bureaucracy and inefficiencies of means-testing. When payments are universal, there is no need for income verification, and recipients are not discouraged from working due to benefit reductions.

• **Critics argue for a targeted approach**, where only low- and middle-income individuals receive UBI, reducing costs and ensuring that the wealthiest citizens do not receive unnecessary payments. However, this introduces administrative complexity and could reduce public support for the program if it is perceived as just another welfare initiative rather than a universal right.

Residency and Citizenship Criteria

Another key question is whether UBI should be restricted to citizens or include long-term residents and immigrants.

• **Citizenship-based UBI** would limit payments to legal citizens of a country. This approach might be politically popular but could exclude long-term residents who contribute to society through work and taxes.

• **Residency-based UBI** could extend payments to all legal residents, ensuring that immigrants and permanent residents receive financial support. However, this raises questions about duration—should someone receive UBI after living in the country for six months? A year? Five years?

• **Temporary and undocumented workers**– One of the most contentious issues is whether UBI should be extended to undocumented immigrants. Some argue that excluding them would push vulnerable populations further into poverty, while others believe it would incentivize illegal immigration and create political backlash.

Most real-world proposals suggest a compromise: UBI payments could be reserved for legal citizens and long-term residents who have lived in the country for a certain number of years, ensuring fairness while preventing abuse of the system.

Who Is Excluded and Why?

Even with a broad definition of eligibility, some individuals or groups might be excluded from receiving UBI. Possible exclusions include:

Minors and Children

Many UBI models propose limiting payments to adults while offering a smaller child benefit for parents or guardians. Providing full UBI to children could dramatically increase costs, though some argue that families with children should receive extra support to reflect the higher cost of raising children.

Incarcerated Individuals

Most UBI proposals suggest suspending payments for individuals serving prison sentences, as their basic needs (housing, food, medical care) are covered by the state. However, payments might resume upon release to help with reintegration.

High-Income Earners

Some proposals suggest phasing out UBI for the wealthiest individuals to reduce costs. This could be achieved through higher taxation rather than direct exclusion, ensuring that high-income earners still receive payments but contribute more in taxes to fund the program.

Non-Residents and Temporary Workers

UBI is generally intended for permanent residents or citizens, meaning that temporary workers, tourists, and short-term expatriates would not be eligible. However, this raises concerns about fairness for migrant workers who contribute to the economy but do not receive the same benefits.

Here's the second chapter of your book on Universal Basic Income.

Chapter 2: Who Qualifies for Universal Basic Income?

Introduction

Universal Basic Income (UBI) is often described as an unconditional payment provided to every citizen, yet the reality of implementing such a system requires careful consideration of eligibility criteria. Would UBI be given to individuals or households? Would there be economic or residency requirements? Who, if anyone, would be excluded? While the "universal" in UBI suggests inclusivity, most real-world proposals introduce some level of qualification to balance cost, effectiveness, and fairness.

This chapter explores how eligibility for UBI might be determined, the potential consequences of different approaches, and the debates surrounding who should and should not receive payments.

Individual vs. Household Eligibility

A major question in designing a UBI system is whether payments should be distributed on an individual basis or determined at the household level. Each approach has distinct advantages and challenges.

Individual Eligibility: The Purest Form of UBI

In a truly universal system, every adult would receive a basic income regardless of their marital status, household structure, or employment situation. This approach ensures maximum simplicity, fairness, and autonomy. Since each person receives the same amount, there is no need for complex calculations based on family size or shared resources.

Advantages of individual UBI:

- **Simplicity**– No need to track household composition.
- **Autonomy** – Payments go directly to individuals rather than being controlled by a spouse or head of household.
- **Avoids marriage or cohabitation penalties**– No reduction in benefits based on household income.

However, some critics argue that distributing UBI solely on an individual basis could create inefficiencies. For example, a household of two working adults would receive double the amount of UBI compared to a single parent raising children alone, even though the latter might have greater financial needs.

Household-Based UBI: A More Cost-Conscious Approach

An alternative approach is to calculate UBI based on household composition. In this model, payments might be structured in a way that provides a reduced per-person amount for those living together, recognizing that households can share costs such as rent, utilities, and food.

Advantages of household-based UBI:

- **Cost efficiency**– Reducing payments for multi-person households could make UBI more affordable.
- **Addresses economies of scale**– Recognizes that shared living arrangements lower individual costs.

However, this model raises several concerns:

- **Increased bureaucracy**– Determining household size and composition adds complexity.
- **Potential marriage penalties** – Couples or roommates might receive lower payments, discouraging cohabitation.
- **Control issues** – In some cases, one member of the household could dominate financial decisions, limiting individual autonomy.

Ultimately, whether UBI should be structured at the individual or household level depends on balancing fairness, economic feasibility, and administrative complexity. Most UBI proposals favor individual eligibility to avoid bureaucratic inefficiencies, even if this increases costs.

Economic and Residency Requirements

Although UBI is often discussed as "universal," most proposals consider placing some conditions on eligibility based on economic status or residency.

Should UBI Be Means-Tested?

One of the most controversial questions about UBI is whether it should be given to everyone regardless of income or reserved for those below a certain economic threshold.

- **Proponents of universal payments** argue that UBI should be unconditional to avoid the bureaucracy and inefficiencies of means-testing. When payments are universal, there is no need for income verification, and recipients are not discouraged from working due to benefit reductions.
- **Critics argue for a targeted approach** where only low- and middle-income individuals receive UBI, reducing costs and ensuring that the wealthiest citizens do not receive unnecessary payments. However, this introduces administrative complexity and could reduce public support for the program if it is perceived as just another welfare initiative rather than a universal right.

Residency and Citizenship Criteria

Another key question is whether UBI should be restricted to citizens or include long-term residents and immigrants.

- **Citizenship-based UBI** would limit payments to legal citizens of a country. This approach might be politically popular but could exclude long-term residents who contribute to society through work and taxes.
- **Residency-based UBI** could extend payments to all legal residents, ensuring that immigrants and permanent residents receive financial support. However, this raises questions about duration—should someone receive UBI after living in the country for six months? A year? Five years?
- **Temporary and undocumented workers**– One of the most contentious issues is whether UBI should be extended to undocumented immigrants. Some argue that excluding them would push vulnerable populations further into poverty, while others believe it would incentivize illegal immigration and create political backlash.

Most real-world proposals suggest a compromise: UBI payments could be reserved for legal citizens and long-term residents who have lived in the country for a certain number of years, ensuring fairness while preventing abuse of the system.

Who Is Excluded and Why?

Even with a broad definition of eligibility, some individuals or groups might be excluded from receiving UBI. Possible exclusions include:

Minors and Children

Many UBI models propose limiting payments to adults while offering a smaller child benefit for parents or guardians. Providing full UBI to children could dramatically increase costs, though some argue that families with children should receive extra support to reflect the higher cost of raising children.

Incarcerated Individuals

Most UBI proposals suggest suspending payments for individuals serving prison sentences, as their basic needs (housing, food, medical care) are covered by the state. However, payments might resume upon release to help with reintegration.

High-Income Earners

Some proposals suggest phasing out UBI for the wealthiest individuals to reduce costs. This could be achieved through higher taxation rather than direct exclusion, ensuring that high-income earners still receive payments but contribute more in taxes to fund the program.

Non-Residents and Temporary Workers

UBI is generally intended for permanent residents or citizens, meaning that temporary workers, tourists, and short-term expatriates would not be eligible. However, this raises concerns about fairness for migrant workers who contribute to the economy but do not receive the same benefits.

Conclusion

Determining who qualifies for UBI is one of the most critical design questions in any basic income system. Should it be given to individuals or adjusted based on household size? Should it be truly universal, or should there be income and residency requirements? While the ideal of UBI is simple—ensuring financial security for all—the practical considerations of eligibility introduce complexities that must be addressed.

Actions and in-actions generate consequences. People and the conditions for living change. As these changes transpire, the conditions for a universal basic income recede. In the next chapter, we will focus on what happens when people are no longer qualified for a UBI.

CHAPTER 3
HOW DO YOU LOSE THE UBI?

Introduction

A key aspect of designing a Universal Basic Income (UBI) system is determining whether and how recipients might lose access to the payments. Would UBI be an unconditional, lifelong benefit, or would certain economic or behavioral conditions lead to disqualification? Should recipients lose their UBI if they reach a certain income threshold? Would there be work requirements, or would UBI be truly "no strings attached"?

This chapter explores the factors that could cause someone to lose their UBI, the philosophical and economic debates surrounding these conditions, and potential phase-out strategies that could ensure the program remains both effective and financially sustainable.

Income Thresholds and Disqualification

While UBI is often envisioned as a universal program, some proposals suggest limiting or phasing out payments for high-income earners. The question then becomes: should UBI have an income threshold that disqualifies recipients once they surpass a certain earnings level?

The Case for Income-Based Disqualification

Some critics argue that UBI should not be given to individuals who do not need it. Under this model, payments would be phased out or eliminated once a recipient reaches a designated income level. Proponents argue that this approach:

- **Reduces program costs** by ensuring that UBI primarily supports those who need it most.
- **Prevents unnecessary government spending** on high-income individuals who already have financial security.
- **Allows UBI to function more like a safety net**, supporting those who experience temporary hardship rather than providing payments to everyone indefinitely.

However, implementing an income-based cutoff introduces bureaucratic challenges, such as requiring income verification, which could lead to inefficiencies similar to traditional welfare programs.

The Case for Unconditional Payments

On the other side of the debate, proponents of truly universal UBI argue that adding income-based restrictions undermines the very purpose of the program. They point out that:

- **Means-testing adds complexity** and increases administrative costs, making the system less efficient.
- **A fixed income threshold could discourage work**, as people may intentionally keep their earnings below the cutoff to continue receiving payments.
- **Universal payments ensure fairness** by treating all citizens equally, rather than creating a tiered system where some qualify and others do not.

One way to balance these concerns is through a **progressive taxation model**, where high-income earners still receive UBI but pay a higher percentage of their earnings back into the system through taxes. This way, everyone benefits from the financial security UBI provides while ensuring that those with greater wealth contribute more.

Behavioral Conditions: Work Requirements or No Strings Attached?

Another contentious issue in UBI policy is whether recipients should have to meet certain behavioral conditions—such as working, seeking employment, or engaging in community service—to continue receiving payments. Traditional welfare programs often include such conditions, but should UBI follow the same model?

The Argument for Work Requirements

Some policymakers believe that UBI should not simply be "free money" and that recipients should be required to contribute to society in some way. This could take the form of:

- **A work requirement**, ensuring recipients are actively employed or seeking employment.

- **Volunteer or community service obligations** where recipients contribute to public projects or nonprofits.
- **Job training or education mandates** requiring recipients to enroll in courses or skill-building programs.

The rationale behind these conditions is to **prevent dependency on government assistance** and ensure that UBI encourages productivity rather than idleness. Some critics worry that, without work requirements, people might choose not to work at all, potentially reducing overall economic output.

The Case for No Strings Attached

The core philosophy behind many UBI proposals is that payments should be **unconditional**—meaning no one is required to work, prove job-seeking efforts, or participate in specific programs to continue receiving funds. Supporters of unconditional UBI argue that:

- **Work requirements create bureaucracy** increasing administrative costs and defeating the simplicity of UBI.
- **UBI allows people to pursue meaningful work** whether or not it is paid. This includes caregiving, entrepreneurship, artistic endeavors, and community engagement.
- **Evidence suggests most people will continue working** even with UBI, using the financial support to transition into better jobs, start businesses, or further their education.

Experiments such as Finland's UBI pilot and Canada's Mincome project showed that **recipients did not stop working**; instead, they used their income to invest in career development, education, and personal well-being.

Ultimately, whether UBI should have behavioral conditions depends on whether it is seen as a welfare replacement (which typically comes with conditions) or a universal right (which should be unconditional).

Potential Phase-Out Strategies

If UBI is not meant to be permanent for everyone, how should it be phased out? There are different models for gradually reducing payments rather than abruptly cutting off individuals when they reach an income threshold.

Tapered Reduction Model

Instead of a strict cutoff, UBI could gradually decrease as recipients earn more money. For example:

- If a person earns below $30,000 per year, they receive the full UBI amount.
- Between $30,000 and $60,000, payments graduallyreduce.
- Above $60,000, payments phase outcompletely.

This approach ensures that individuals do not suddenly lose financial support, which could discourage them from seeking higher-paying jobs.

Taxation-Based Recapture

A more seamless way to phase out UBI is through **progressive taxation** rather than direct benefit reduction. Under this model, everyone receives UBI, but higher earners contribute a greater portion of their income back into the system through taxes.

For example, if UBI is funded by a flat 10% tax on all income, individuals making $100,000 per year would pay significantly more in taxes than those earning $20,000, effectively "returning" their UBI to the system.

Time-Limited UBI

Some proposals suggest that UBI should not be a lifelong benefit but rather a temporary measure for individuals during economic hardship, career transitions, or job loss. In this model:

- UBI could be **age-restricted**, such as providing payments only to individuals between 18-65 years old.
- UBI could be **time-limited**, such as a guaranteed income for five years per person, allowing recipients to use it strategically.

However, critics argue that limiting UBI in this way **undermines its security and simplicity**, making it more like traditional welfare programs rather than a true universal benefit.

Conclusion

While UBI is often framed as a permanent, universal benefit, there are many debates about whether recipients should be disqualified under certain conditions. Should people lose UBI if they earn too much money? Should work or community service be required to continue receiving payments? Should payments be phased out gradually or through taxation?

These questions reveal the core tensions in UBI policy: balancing universality with affordability, simplicity with fairness, and individual autonomy with economic responsibility. The answers will ultimately depend on political will, economic feasibility, and societal values.

As we continue to explore the feasibility of UBI, the next chapter will examine how it could be funded. Where would the money come from to sustain a universal income? Would new taxes be necessary, or could existing welfare programs be restructured? Understanding the financial implications of UBI is crucial to assessing whether it is a practical solution or an economic impossibility.

CHAPTER 4
FUNDING UBI: WHERE DOES THE MONEY COME FROM?

Introduction

One of the most common criticisms of Universal Basic Income (UBI) is its cost. While the idea of providing every citizen with a guaranteed income is appealing, the central question remains: **where does the money come from?** Opponents argue that UBI is too expensive and unsustainable, while supporters believe it can be funded through innovative taxation, economic growth, and reallocation of existing government spending.

This chapter explores the most discussed funding methods for UBI, including taxation, redirection of welfare spending, and the potential revenue generated from automation-driven economic growth.

Taxation: Wealth Tax, VAT, Carbon Tax, and More

Raising revenue through taxation is one of the most direct ways to fund UBI. Several types of taxes have been proposed as potential sources, each with its own advantages and drawbacks.

Wealth Tax: Targeting the Richest 1%

A **wealth tax** is a tax on an individual's net worth, including assets such as real estate, stocks, and cash holdings.

- **How it works:** A small percentage (e.g., 1-3%) is levied annually on wealth above a certain threshold (e.g., $10 million).

- **Potential revenue:** Estimates suggest a wealth tax could generate **hundreds of billions of dollars per year** in the U.S. alone.
- **Pros:** Targets those who have benefited most from economic growth; could reduce wealth inequality.
- **Cons:** Could lead to capital flight if the ultra-wealthy move assets offshore; administrative challenges in valuing non-liquid assets.

Countries like France and Sweden experimented with wealth taxes but faced challenges enforcing them. However, with improved global tax coordination, a wealth tax could be a viable tool for funding UBI.

Value-Added Tax (VAT): Broadening the Tax Base

A **Value-Added Tax (VAT)** is a consumption tax applied to goods and services at each stage of production. Many European countries use VAT to fund public programs.

- **How it works:**A small percentage (e.g., 10-20%) is added to the price of goods and services.
- **Potential revenue:**A 10% VAT in the U.S. could generate over **$1 trillion per year**.
- **Pros:** Harder to evade than income taxes; taxes spending rather than earnings.
- **Cons:**Regressive—disproportionately affects lower-income individuals.

One way to offset VAT's regressive impact is to **exempt essential goods** (e.g., food, medicine) and use a portion of the revenue to ensure UBI benefits the poor more than the rich.

Carbon Tax: Making Polluters Pay

A **carbon tax** imposes a fee on fossil fuel consumption, discouraging emissions and funding public programs.

- **How it works:** Companies and consumers pay a tax on carbon-based fuels (coal, oil, natural gas).
- **Potential revenue:**A carbon tax of $50 per ton could generate **$200-300 billion annually in the U.S.**
- **Pros:** Encourages green energy transition; reduces environmental damage.
- **Cons:**Could raise energy prices; requires global cooperation to prevent businesses from relocating to low-tax countries.

Some UBI proposals, like the **Alaska Permanent Fund**, already use a resource tax model—Alaska distributes oil revenue as dividends to residents. A national carbon tax could fund a similar approach.

Financial Transaction Tax (FTT): A Small Fee on Wall Street

An **FTT** applies a small tax (e.g., 0.1%) on financial trades, such as stock, bond, and derivatives transactions.

- **Potential revenue:** Some estimates suggest an FTT could raise **$60-100 billion annually** in the U.S.
- **Pros:** Targets high-frequency trading and speculation; has minimal impact on ordinary investors.
- **Cons:** Could reduce market liquidity; financial institutions might pass costs to consumers.

Countries like France and Italy have implemented versions of an FTT, showing that it is a feasible revenue source.

Redirecting Existing Welfare Spending

Another way to fund UBI is by **consolidating and repurposing existing welfare programs**. Instead of multiple targeted assistance programs, the government could replace them with a single universal payment.

Eliminating Redundant Welfare Programs

Governments already spend billions on welfare, food assistance, housing subsidies, and unemployment benefits. A UBI could simplify these programs by providing direct cash payments instead.

- **U.S. example:** The U.S. spends over **$1 trillion per year** on welfare and anti-poverty programs. If UBI replaced some of these programs, the additional funding required would be significantly lower than the total cost of UBI.
- **Pros:** Reduces administrative costs; eliminates bureaucratic inefficiencies.
- **Cons:** Some vulnerable groups (e.g., disabled individuals, seniors) might need additional support beyond UBI.

Defense Budget Reallocation

Many governments, particularly the U.S., spend massive amounts on military defense. A small reduction in defense spending could free up funds for UBI.

- **Example:** The U.S. defense budget is **$800+ billion per year**—even a **10% cut** could provide significant funding.
- **Pros:** Redirects spending toward domestic well-being rather than warfare.
- **Cons:** Faces strong political resistance; national security concerns.

. . .

The Role of Automation and Economic Growth

One of the most compelling arguments for UBI is that **automation is replacing human jobs**, making a guaranteed income necessary for economic stability.

Automation and the "Robot Tax"

As AI and robots take over jobs, governments could impose a **robot tax**—a fee on companies that replace human workers with automation.

- **How it works:**Companies pay a tax on automation-related job losses.
- **Potential revenue:** Could generate **hundreds of billions annually** as automation expands.
- **Pros:** Encourages companies to create new jobs or fund UBI as compensation.
- **Cons:** Could discourage technological innovation if tax rates are too high.

Bill Gates has suggested a robot tax to ensure that companies profiting from automation contribute to worker support systems.

Economic Growth and Increased Productivity

UBI could also be self-funding **if it boosts economic activity**. When people have a stable income, they:

- **Spend more**, increasing demand for goods and services.
- **Invest in education**, leading to a more skilled workforce.
- **Start businesses**, creating jobs and boosting entrepreneurship.

A **stronger economy leads to higher tax revenues**, which can further sustain UBI without requiring drastic tax hikes.

Conclusion

Funding UBI is not an impossible challenge—it requires a mix of creative taxation, reallocation of existing resources, and harnessing the benefits of automation-driven economic growth. From wealth taxes to carbon taxes, from VAT to financial transaction taxes, and from cutting unnecessary bureaucracy to leveraging automation, there are multiple viable pathways to fund a universal basic income.

The real question is not whether UBI is affordable, but **whether society has the political will to prioritize financial security for all**.

In the next chapter, we will explore one of the most important questions about UBI: **how do we pay for it?** Understanding the funding mechanisms behind UBI is critical to assessing its long-term sustainability.

CHAPTER 5
IS UBI AFFORDABLE

Introduction

One of the biggest concerns surrounding Universal Basic Income (UBI) is affordability. Can governments sustain a program that guarantees a regular income to every citizen? Critics argue that UBI is too expensive, would strain national budgets, and could lead to higher taxes or inflation. Supporters counter that UBI can be funded through taxation, economic growth, and efficiency gains by consolidating existing welfare programs.

This chapter explores UBI's financial feasibility by examining its impact on government budgets, comparing it to current social safety nets, and assessing the long-term cost of **not** implementing UBI in the face of rising inequality, automation-driven job losses, and economic instability.

Government Budget Impact and Sustainability

How Much Would UBI Cost?

The cost of UBI depends on three factors:

1 **The payment amount**– A modest UBI might be $12,000 per year per adult, while a more ambitious version could be higher.

2 **Who receives it**– Universal (everyone) vs. targeted (only those below a certain income level).

3 **Funding sources** – Whether new taxes, budget reallocations, or economic growth offset the cost.

For example, in the United States:

- A UBI of**$12,000 per year for every adult** (about 250 million people) would cost approximately **$3 trillion annually**.
- A UBI that**excludes the wealthiest 20%** could reduce costs to around **$2 trillion annually**.
- A**partial UBI**—providing a smaller amount or targeting specific groups—could cost significantly less.

Can Governments Afford UBI?

The U.S. government alone **already spends over $5 trillion per year** on various programs, including welfare, Social Security, healthcare, and military. A well-designed UBI could be **partially funded by redirecting existing spending** and increasing taxes on wealth, financial transactions, or automation-driven corporate profits.

In addition, UBI could generate **new tax revenue** by boosting economic activity. If people spend their UBI on goods and services, businesses earn more, leading to increased tax collection through sales tax, income tax, and corporate tax.

Comparing UBI to Existing Social Safety Nets

Many governments already have complex social safety nets, including:

- Unemploymentbenefits
- Food assistance programs (SNAP,WIC)
- Housingsubsidies
- Disabilitysupport
- SocialSecurity

These programs **target specific groups** but often come with bureaucratic inefficiencies, high administrative costs, and gaps where people fall through the cracks.

UBI vs. Traditional Welfare

Factor

UBI

Traditional Welfare

Eligibility

Universal or simple income-based threshold

Complex requirements, means-tested

Administrative Cost

Lower – automatic payments to all

Higher – bureaucratic oversight needed

Stigma

None – received by everyone

High – seen as "handouts"

Work Incentive

Encourages entrepreneurship & part-time work

Can discourage work due to benefit phase-out

Fraud Risk

Low – no complicated eligibility checks

Higher – requires oversight & enforcement

Many argue that **UBI would simplify government spending**, replacing inefficient programs with direct cash payments. Countries like Finland and Canada have tested basic income programs, showing that direct cash transfers can be more effective at reducing poverty and improving well-being.

However, some welfare programs—such as disability assistance—may still need to exist alongside UBI for those with additional needs.

The Cost of Doing Nothing: Rising Inequality, Job Loss, and Instability

Critics of UBI focus on its price tag, but **failing to implement solutions for economic inequality could be far more costly** in the long run.

Rising Wealth Inequality

Wealth is becoming increasingly concentrated in the hands of a few, while wages for the middle and lower classes stagnate. Without intervention:

- **Poverty will deepen**, increasing reliance on emergency aid, food banks, and unstable gig work.
- **Social unrest may rise**, as economic inequality has historically been linked to protests and political instability.
- **Government spending on crime, healthcare, and homelessness could increase**, offsetting any savings from rejecting UBI.

Automation and Job Loss

AI and automation are rapidly eliminating traditional jobs. Self-driving trucks, AI customer service, and robotic manufacturing could displace **millions** of workers in the coming decades. Without UBI:

- Many displaced workers may **struggle to retrain or find stable employment**.

- Increased job precarity could **reduce consumer spending**, slowing economic growth.
- Governments may face **higher unemployment costs and welfare demands**, making inaction even more expensive.

Economic Instability and Recession Risks

A weak consumer base—caused by low wages, job loss, and inequality—can **slow economic growth and trigger recessions.**

- **UBI could act as an economic stabilizer**by ensuring that everyone has purchasing power, keeping businesses afloat.
- Studies suggest that direct cash payments increase demand for goods and services, driving GDP growth.
- **Without UBI, we risk a future where only the wealthy benefit from automation-driven profits, while the majority struggle to afford basic needs.**

Conclusion: Is UBI Affordable?

The question **isn't just whether UBI is affordable, but whether we can afford not to implement it.**

- **UBI is costly, but not impossible**—it can be funded through taxation, redirected spending, and economic growth.
- **UBI could replace inefficient welfare programs**, reducing bureaucracy and administrative costs.
- **The cost of inaction—rising inequality, unemployment, and economic instability—could be far greater than UBI's price tag.**

The real challenge is **political will.** Governments can afford UBI if they prioritize fair taxation, economic sustainability, and long-term prosperity over short-term concerns.

In the next chapter, we will explore the difference between UBI and how welfare is used to support people who can't meet their needs. How can we make a society where all people can maximize their contribution to society when they no longer have to endlessly toil and still not be able to pay for rent, healthcare, transportation and education? Is the answer UBI or welfare or both?

CHAPTER 6
UBI VS. TRADITIONAL WELFARE

Introduction

Universal Basic Income (UBI) is often framed as an alternative or a replacement for traditional welfare programs. Advocates of UBI argue that it is a **simpler, fairer, and more efficient** way to provide financial security. Opponents, however, claim that traditional welfare is **more targeted and cost-effective**, ensuring that resources go to those who need them the most.

This chapter explores the **key differences** between UBI and traditional welfare, examines the arguments on both sides, and discusses whether these two approaches to economic security can coexist or if one should replace the other.

Key Differences in Structure and Purpose

Universal Basic Income (UBI)

UBI is **unconditional cash assistance** provided to all individuals, regardless of employment status, wealth, or other circumstances. The key characteristics include:

- **Universal:** Everyone receives it, eliminating complex eligibility requirements.
- **Unconditional:**No work requirements or restrictions on how the money is spent.

- **Regular and Guaranteed:**Payments are predictable and consistent.
- **Simplified Administration:** Because it is automatic, it requires less bureaucracy than welfare programs.

The main goal of UBI is to provide **a financial floor for everyone,** ensuring that no one falls into absolute poverty. It is designed to **support economic freedom**, allowing people to pursue education, entrepreneurship, or flexible work arrangements without worrying about survival.

Traditional Welfare

Welfare programs are **means-tested**, meaning they are provided only to individuals who meet specific eligibility criteria based on income, employment status, disability, or family circumstances. Welfare programs often include:

- **Food assistance (SNAP,WIC)**
- **Housing subsidies (Section 8, publichousing)**
- **Unemploymentbenefits**
- **Disability payments (SSI,SSDI)**
- **Healthcare assistance (Medicaid, Medicaresubsidies)**

The purpose of welfare is to **target resources where they are needed most**, ensuring that limited government funds go to the most vulnerable populations. However, welfare programs often come with **eligibility restrictions, work requirements, and administrative hurdles** that can prevent some people from receiving aid when they need it.

Comparison Factor

UBI

Traditional Welfare

Eligibility

Everyone

Means-tested (only those below income thresholds qualify)

Work Requirements

None

Often required

Purpose

Economic stability and individual freedom

Targeted assistance for poverty relief

Administration

Simple, automatic payments

Complex bureaucracy and oversight needed

Stigma

None, since everyone receives it
Can carry social stigma as "handouts"
Fraud Risk
Low, as everyone gets the same amount
Higher due to eligibility verification requirements

Why Do Some Argue UBI is Better?

1. UBI Eliminates Bureaucracy and Administrative Costs

Traditional welfare programs require **eligibility verification, application processes, and enforcement mechanisms**. This means government agencies must process applications, check incomes, investigate fraud, and manage payments.

By contrast, UBI is **simple**: Every citizen receives it **without paperwork, caseworkers, or compliance checks**. This dramatically reduces administrative costs and government inefficiencies.

2. UBI Encourages Work, Entrepreneurship, and Innovation

Critics of traditional welfare argue that it can create **"welfare traps"**—meaning that recipients fear taking a job or earning more money because they might lose their benefits.

UBI **does not phase out based on income**, meaning people can work, start businesses, or pursue education **without risking their financial security**. This encourages entrepreneurship and economic participation rather than discouraging it.

3. UBI Provides Dignity and Freedom

Welfare programs often restrict how recipients can use their benefits. For example, food stamps can only be spent on groceries, and housing vouchers can only be used for specific landlords. UBI, on the other hand, allows people to **spend money based on their own needs**, restoring financial independence.

Additionally, welfare programs often carry **stigma**, as recipients are sometimes viewed as "lazy" or "dependent." Since UBI is universal, it avoids these negative perceptions.

4. UBI Prepares Society for Automation and Job Displacement

As automation eliminates millions of jobs in industries like transportation, retail, and customer service, **UBI provides a safety net for workers displaced by technological change**. Unlike welfare, which reacts to hardship after it happens, UBI **proactively ensures financial stability before people fall into poverty**.

Why Do Others Say Welfare is More Targeted and Effective?

1. UBI is Expensive and Could Drain Resources from Those in Need

One major criticism of UBI is that **it gives money to everyone—even those who don't need it**. If billionaires receive the same basic income as the poor, critics argue that **precious government resources could be better spent targeting aid where it is truly needed**.

Instead of providing universal payments, some believe that **strengthening existing welfare programs**—such as expanding food assistance, affordable housing, and unemployment benefits—would be a more cost-effective way to help those in need.

2. Traditional Welfare Provides Greater Support for the Most Vulnerable

Some people need **more than just cash assistance**. Individuals with disabilities, single parents, and those experiencing long-term unemployment **may require additional support services, such as job training, mental health care, or childcare subsidies**—things that UBI alone cannot provide.

Welfare programs offer specialized aid that UBI **may not replace effectively**.

3. UBI Does Not Address Structural Inequality

Critics argue that **poverty is not just about income—it is about access to opportunities, education, healthcare, and stable housing**.

For example, if someone receives $1,000 per month in UBI but still cannot afford rent in a high-cost city, they may remain in poverty. Traditional welfare programs aim to address these structural barriers by **providing direct aid in areas such as housing, job placement, and healthcare**.

4. Could UBI Replace Welfare Without Sufficient Safety Nets?

Some fear that if UBI were implemented, governments might use it as an excuse to **cut welfare programs entirely**, leaving the most vulnerable worse off. For example, if a UBI payment is too small to cover all essential expenses, but welfare programs are eliminated, low-income individuals might actually be **worse off under UBI than under a strong social safety net**.

. . .

Can UBI and Welfare Coexist?

UBI and traditional welfare do not have to be mutually exclusive. Some proposals suggest a **hybrid model**, where:

- UBI provides a basic income floor foreveryone.
- Targeted welfare programs continue for those with additional needs (such as disability or housing assistance).
- Social services like**healthcare, job training, and education remain fully funded**.

In this model, UBI simplifies cash assistance, while welfare continues to provide essential services to those who need them.

Conclusion: Which Approach is Better?

There is no single answer to whether UBI or traditional welfare is the better system.

- **UBI is simpler, universal, and eliminates bureaucracy**, but it is expensive and may not fully address the needs of the most vulnerable.
- **Traditional welfare is targeted and cost-effective**, but it can be complex, stigmatizing, and create work disincentives.

Ultimately, the best approach may be a **combination of both**—using UBI to provide a financial foundation for all, while maintaining essential support programs for those who need additional help.

Next Chapter: In the next chapter, we will explore the economic impact of UBI: Would it cause inflation? Would people stop working? Would it stimulate economic growth? Understanding these effects is crucial in assessing whether UBI is a sustainable long-term solution.

CHAPTER 7
ECONOMIC IMPACT OF UNIVERSAL BASIC INCOME

Introduction

One of the most debated aspects of Universal Basic Income (UBI) is its potential impact on the economy. Would it lead to widespread unemployment, or would it empower people to seek better opportunities? Would it cause runaway inflation, or would it stimulate growth? Would it encourage entrepreneurship and innovation, or create complacency?

This chapter examines the economic effects of UBI, focusing on how it might influence **employment, wages, inflation, and entrepreneurship**, and whether it would strengthen or weaken local economies.

Effects on Employment and Wages

One of the biggest concerns about UBI is whether people would continue to work if they received a guaranteed income. Opponents argue that **free money could reduce incentives to work**, leading to labor shortages and lower productivity. Supporters, on the other hand, suggest that **UBI could increase workforce participation** by reducing financial stress and allowing people to pursue better opportunities.

Would UBI Make People Stop Working?

Evidence from pilot programs suggests that **most people do not stop**

working when they receive a basic income. Instead, they use it as a financial cushion to:

- **Switch to better jobs** – People trapped in low-paying or exploitative jobs may use UBI to seek better opportunities.
- **Pursue education or training** – With financial security, people can invest in their skills and qualifications.
- **Start businesses** – UBI can provide the initial capital needed to take entrepreneurial risks.
- **Improve work-life balance**– Some may reduce working hours to spend time with family, but this does not mean they become unproductive.

Studies from **Finland's UBI experiment (2017-2018)** showed that while employment levels remained steady, recipients reported **greater well-being and motivation to seek better jobs**. Similarly, the **Canada Mincome experiment (1974-1979)** found that only two groups significantly reduced working hours: **students (who stayed in school longer) and new mothers (who cared for children at home).**

Impact on Wages

UBI could have two contrasting effects on wages:

1 **Higher wages for undesirable jobs**– If UBI gives workers more financial security, they may refuse low-wage jobs with poor conditions, forcing employers to offer **higher wages** and better benefits to attract workers.

2 **Lower wages for desirable jobs** – Some workers might be willing to accept lower wages in jobs they enjoy, knowing they have a financial safety net. This could impact fields like **arts, social work, and education**, where passion-driven workers might be willing to work for less.

Ultimately, UBI **shifts bargaining power toward workers**, giving them more freedom to choose work that aligns with their skills, values, and interests.

Inflation Concerns: Real or Exaggerated?

A common fear is that UBI could cause **inflation**, meaning that if everyone has more money, prices will rise, negating the benefits of the program. While this concern is valid, it depends on how UBI is structured and funded.

Would UBI Lead to Higher Prices?

Inflation occurs when there is **too much money chasing too few goods**. If UBI simply prints new money without increasing production, inflation could result. However, if UBI is funded through **redistribution (taxes, automation revenue, etc.) rather than money creation**, inflationary effects may be limited.

Housing and Rent Inflation

One sector that could experience inflation is **housing**. If people have more money, landlords might **raise rents**, making housing even more unaffordable. Solutions could include **rent controls, increased housing supply, or targeted housing policies** alongside UBI.

Automation and Productivity Growth as Counterbalance

If UBI allows people to **pursue education, start businesses, or participate in more productive activities**, it could actually **increase economic output**, offsetting inflationary effects. The key is ensuring that UBI is implemented alongside policies that support **innovation, investment, and production growth**.

Boosting Entrepreneurship and Local Economies

One of the strongest arguments for UBI is its potential to **stimulate entrepreneurship and small business growth**.

How UBI Encourages Entrepreneurship

Starting a business is risky, and financial insecurity often prevents people from taking the leap. With UBI, individuals have a safety net that allows them to:

- **Take business risks**– Without the fear of complete financial ruin, more people may be willing to start companies.
- **Cover initial expenses**– UBI can act as a form of seed funding, helping small businesses get off the ground.
- **Experiment with new ideas**– Innovators and creatives may have the freedom to explore ideas without immediate financial pressure.

Research suggests that when people have basic financial security, **entrepreneurial activity increases**. In the **Cherokee Nation's basic income experiment**, which provided unconditional cash payments to Native American tribal members, new business creation **rose by 15%**.

Strengthening Local Economies

UBI ensures that money is consistently flowing into communities, which can boost local businesses and stimulate **economic activity from the ground up**. When people have disposable income, they are more likely to:

- **Support local businesses** instead of relying on cheap, mass-produced goods.
- **Invest in their communities** leading to greater economic stability.
- **Increase consumer spending** driving demand for goods and services.

Instead of wealth being concentrated in large corporations and the financial sector, UBI **redistributes money directly to consumers, fueling grassroots economic growth**.

Conclusion: A Net Positive or a Risky Experiment?

The economic effects of UBI depend on **how it is designed and implemented**.

- **Employment & Wages** – While some might reduce working hours, evidence suggests that UBI **does not discourage work**; instead, it gives people the flexibility to seek better opportunities. Wages may rise for undesirable jobs but could fall in passion-driven fields.
- **Inflation** – If UBI is **funded responsibly**, inflation is unlikely to be a major problem. However, sectors like housing could experience price increases, requiring complementary policies.
- **Entrepreneurship & Local Economies** – UBI could stimulate business creation, boost consumer spending, and strengthen local economies, leading to **long-term economic growth**.

While there are risks, the potential benefits of UBI—greater financial stability, increased innovation, and a more dynamic economy—make it an idea worth considering.

In the next chapter, we will explore one of the most important questions about UBI: **how do we pay for it?**Understanding the funding mechanisms behind UBI is critical to assessing its long-term sustainability.

CHAPTER 8
DO PEOPLE WANT TO PAY FOR UBI?

Introduction

Universal Basic Income (UBI) is often framed as an economic or social policy, but at its core, it is also a question of **public willingness.** Would people be willing to pay higher taxes or shift government spending to fund UBI? Would businesses accept new taxes or economic adjustments to support a basic income? And how does public opinion change when people actually start receiving UBI payments?

This chapter explores public attitudes toward UBI, the **political and cultural factors** that shape those views, and what history tells us about how opinions shift when UBI becomes a reality.

Public Opinion on Taxation for UBI

Funding UBI requires money—either through **higher taxes, redirected government spending, or new revenue sources** like automation or carbon taxes. But are people willing to pay for it?

Polling and Public Sentiment

Surveys on UBI consistently show **mixed but evolving** public opinion:

• **Support varies by country and culture** – In some countries, where social welfare is already strong (e.g., **Finland, Canada, and parts of Europe**), support for UBI is higher. In countries where social assistance is stigmatized (e.g., **the U.S.**), UBI is more controversial.

- **People like the idea but worry about costs**– Many individuals support the concept of UBI but become skeptical when taxation is mentioned.
- **Younger generations tend to be more supportive** – Studies indicate that **Millennials and Gen Z** are more open to UBI, possibly due to their experiences with economic instability, automation, and job market shifts.

A 2020 **Pew Research poll** found that **support for UBI was 45% in the U.S., but among younger adults (ages 18–34), it was over 60%**. Meanwhile, in a 2023 **European survey**, over **70% of respondents in Spain and Portugal supported a UBI**, compared to **less than 50% in Germany and France**.

How Do People Feel About Taxing the Wealthy for UBI?

One of the most common proposals for funding UBI is a **wealth tax**, where the ultra-rich pay a higher share. Polls suggest that:

- **Wealth taxes are broadly popular**, even among those skeptical of UBI.
- **Middle-class taxpayers worry about being affected** even if taxes are only targeted at the top 1%.
- **Businesses and high-income individuals strongly oppose it**, fearing economic consequences.

While taxing the rich may seem like an easy solution, **the reality is more complex**—governments must design tax policies that do not lead to capital flight or economic disruption.

Political Divides and Cultural Attitudes

Left vs. Right Views on UBI

UBI attracts both **progressives and libertarians**, but for different reasons:

- **Progressives (left-leaning individuals)** see UBI as a way to **reduce poverty, improve economic security, and replace outdated welfare systems.**
- **Libertarians (right-leaning individuals)**like UBI because it **eliminates bureaucracy, reduces government intervention, and gives individuals more financial freedom.**
- **Conservatives** often oppose UBI, fearing it will **increase government spending, discourage work, and lead to dependency**.

In the **United States**, UBI proposals have received support from figures across the spectrum, from **Bernie Sanders (left)** to **Andrew Yang (centrist**

tech entrepreneur) and even **Milton Friedman (right-leaning economist, who supported a form of basic income called a Negative Income Tax).**

Cultural Attitudes Toward "Free Money"

How a society views **work, individual responsibility, and government aid** plays a major role in UBI's acceptance:

- **Nordic countries**– Strong social safety nets make UBI a natural extension of existing policies.
- **U.S. & U.K.**– Strong cultural emphasis on self-reliance makes unconditional payments controversial.
- **Asia**– Countries like Japan and South Korea are exploring UBI due to **aging populations and automation risks**.
- **Developing nations**– UBI is seen as a way to **reduce extreme poverty**, with pilots in Kenya, India, and Brazil showing promise.

Cultural narratives about **"deserving" vs. "undeserving" recipients** also shape opinions. If UBI is seen as a way to help struggling workers, it gains support. If it is seen as a **"handout" for the lazy, it faces backlash**.

What Happens When People Start Receiving Free Money?

Shifts in Public Perception

One of the most interesting aspects of UBI is that **opinions often change when people experience it firsthand**.

- **In pilot programs, skepticism turns into support**– Many UBI experiments have shown that even **initially skeptical participants** become strong supporters after receiving payments.
- **People realize it doesn't destroy work ethic**– Recipients continue to work, start businesses, and improve their lives.
- **The economic benefits become visible**– Local economies often experience growth as people spend their UBI on goods and services.

For example, in the **Alaska Permanent Fund**, which gives all residents a yearly dividend from oil revenues, opposition **decreased over time** as Alaskans saw the benefits. Similarly, in a **Kenyan UBI experiment**, recipients became **more entrepreneurial and healthier**, changing perceptions about government aid.

Does "Free Money" Change Behavior?

A common fear is that UBI could make people lazy, encourage drug use, or reduce motivation. However, research shows the opposite:

- **UBI can reduce stress and improve mental health** leading to better decision-making.
- **People use the money to improve their lives** not waste it—many invest in education, job training, or small businesses.
- **Crime rates tend to decrease**when financial insecurity is reduced.

In the **Stockton, California UBI experiment (2019-2021)**, participants **were more likely to find full-time employment** than non-recipients, challenging the myth that UBI discourages work.

Conclusion: Will People Accept UBI?

Public willingness to **pay for UBI** depends on many factors:

- **Framing matters**– If UBI is framed as an investment in economic security rather than a welfare handout, support increases.
- **Experience changes opinions**– Once people receive UBI and see its benefits, they become more supportive.
- **Political and cultural divides remain**– Some societies will embrace UBI faster than others based on their views on taxation, work, and social support.

Ultimately, support for UBI **grows over time**, especially when people see it in action. However, getting to that point requires overcoming political resistance, cultural skepticism, and concerns about affordability.

Next Chapter: Would UBI Make People Lazy and Dependent?

One of the biggest criticisms of UBI is that it could **reduce motivation to work and encourage laziness**. But is this fear backed by evidence? In the next chapter, we will explore how financial security affects human behavior, productivity, and social well-being.

CHAPTER 9
WOULD A UNIVERSAL BASIC INCOME MAKE PEOPLE LAZY?

Introduction

One of the most common critiques of Universal Basic Income (UBI) is that it would make people lazy. Opponents argue that if individuals receive money without working, they will stop seeking employment, become dependent on government aid, and ultimately contribute less to society. This concern is deeply rooted in cultural ideas about **work ethic, personal responsibility, and economic incentives**.

But does receiving a guaranteed income actually reduce motivation? Or is this just a myth? This chapter explores real-world evidence from UBI experiments, its impact on work ethic, and the psychological effects of financial security.

The Myth vs. Reality from Real-World Studies

Despite widespread fears that UBI would encourage laziness, **numerous experiments and pilot programs suggest otherwise**. In fact, many studies show that **UBI can improve employment outcomes, increase entrepreneurship, and boost productivity** rather than discourage work.

Key Studies on UBI and Employment

1. The Stockton, California Experiment (2019–2021)

• In Stockton, 125 randomly selected residents received **$500 per month** for two years.

• **Employment actually increased**—UBI recipients were **twice as likely** to find full-time work compared to non-recipients.

• Many used the money to **invest in job training, stabilize their finances, and reduce stress**, allowing them to be more productive.

2. The Finland UBI Trial (2017–2018)

• Finland provided **2,000 unemployed individuals** with **€560 per month** unconditionally.

• Compared to a control group, UBI recipients **experienced better mental health and reported higher motivation** to work.

• While employment rates remained stable, recipients had **greater life satisfaction** and pursued **more meaningful work**.

3. The Kenya UBI Experiment (2017–Present)

• A large-scale study by the nonprofit **GiveDirectly** gave thousands of Kenyans a **long-term guaranteed income**.

• Instead of reducing work effort, recipients **became more entrepreneurial**—starting businesses, improving farms, and even **working longer hours** because of financial stability.

Across different continents and economic backgrounds, these studies **consistently refute the idea that UBI leads to widespread laziness**. Instead, it often leads to **smarter financial decisions, better job opportunities, and improved well-being**.

Drug Use, Work Ethic, and Social Behavior

One of the biggest fears about UBI is that people will **spend free money on alcohol, drugs, or other destructive behaviors**. However, research suggests that **financial stability actually reduces substance abuse rather than increases it**.

1. Does UBI Lead to More Drug Use?

• A 2016 **World Bank study** found that **cash transfer programs in developing countries** did **not** lead to increased spending on alcohol or tobacco.

• The Stockton UBI trial showed that **participants spent the majority of their funds on necessities**, such as **food, housing, and transportation**.

• The Alaska Permanent Fund, which gives every Alaskan an annual dividend, **has not led to a rise in substance abuse rates**.

2. How Does Financial Stability Impact Work Ethic?

- Stress from financial instability can make people **less productive and more likely to engage in risky behaviors.**
- When people have a financial safety net, they can**make better long-term decisions**, whether it's finding a better job, furthering their education, or starting a business.
- A UBI does not remove the need to work—it gives people**more agency** over how and where they work.

3. Does UBI Lead to Stronger Social Behavior?

- Studies show that financial security**increases civic engagement**—people are **more likely to volunteer, vote, and participate in community activities** when they are not struggling to survive.
- In Kenya's UBI experiment, recipients**invested in their communities**, creating **better local economies** rather than withdrawing from society.
- UBI reduces the stress that leads to**domestic violence, poor health, and family instability**, helping to create **stronger social connections.**

Bottom line: Rather than causing laziness or drug addiction, UBI can actually improve decision-making, increase personal responsibility, and create stronger communities.

The Psychological Effects of Financial Security

Most arguments against UBI focus on **economic incentives**, but they often ignore the **psychological** benefits of financial security.

1. How Financial Stress Impacts the Brain

- Living in poverty **lowers cognitive function**—a famous 2013 study found that financial stress can **reduce IQ by 13 points**, equivalent to **losing a night of sleep.**
- People under financial stress are**more likely to make short-term decisions**, such as taking bad loans or staying in low-paying jobs, instead of thinking about long-term success.
- A basic income provides **mental relief**, allowing people to plan better and make **more productive choices.**

2. How UBI Boosts Productivity

- When people aren't constantly worried about survival, they can**focus on education, skill-building, and creative pursuits.**

- Many UBI recipients use their money to**train for higher-paying jobs** or **start businesses**, rather than quit working.
- A guaranteed income can lead to**better mental health, fewer sick days, and more engaged workers**.

3. UBI and Human Dignity

- A UBI recognizes that**financial security is a basic human right**, not just a reward for labor.
- People perform **better when they feel valued and respected**—this is why countries with strong social safety nets often have **happier and more productive citizens**.
- When individuals are not trapped in poverty, they can**reach their full potential and contribute more to society**.

Conclusion: The Evidence is Clear

The idea that UBI would make people lazy is largely a **myth**. Real-world studies show that **employment levels remain stable or even increase**, people do **not** waste money on drugs or alcohol, and **financial security improves productivity and mental health**.

The real question is not whether UBI makes people lazy, but whether **our current system is holding people back** by keeping them trapped in financial instability. If we want a **more innovative, entrepreneurial, and healthy society**, ensuring basic economic security could be one of the most effective ways to achieve it.

Next Chapter: Why Do Some People Want a No-Strings-Attached UBI?

If UBI doesn't make people lazy, why do some advocates insist that it should come with **no work requirements, conditions, or restrictions**? The next chapter will explore why a **truly unconditional** UBI may be the most effective approach.

CHAPTER 10
WHY NO STRINGS ATTACHED?

Introduction

One of the defining features of Universal Basic Income (UBI) is that it is **unconditional**—every eligible person receives the payment regardless of employment status, income level, or personal circumstances. Critics argue that a UBI without restrictions could lead to misuse or discourage work. However, proponents contend that adding conditions would **increase bureaucracy, create inefficiencies, and ultimately undermine the very purpose of UBI**.

This chapter explores why a **no-strings-attached** approach to UBI might be the most effective, focusing on the **administrative costs of enforcing restrictions**, whether conditional programs **create unnecessary bureaucracy**, and how restrictions **impact recipients**.

The Administrative Cost of Enforcing Restrictions

Governments already run numerous social welfare programs with strict eligibility requirements, and **the cost of enforcing those restrictions is significant**. Programs like unemployment benefits, food assistance, and disability aid require **extensive monitoring, verification, and enforcement**—all of which come with a price tag.

1. The Cost of Policing Eligibility

When a government imposes conditions on financial aid, it must ensure that:

- **Only those who meet the criteria receivebenefits.**
- **Recipients continue to meet the criteria overtime.**
- **Fraudulent claims are investigated andprevented.**

This requires a **large bureaucratic infrastructure**, including:

- Caseworkers to**review applications and verify eligibility**.
- Auditors to**monitor compliance** and prevent fraud.
- Legal teams to**handle disputes and appeals** when applicants are denied benefits.

For example, in the United States, the **Supplemental Nutrition Assistance Program (SNAP)**, commonly known as food stamps, spends **billions of dollars annually** on administrative costs alone—just to determine who qualifies and ensure compliance. **Wouldn't it be more efficient to simply provide everyone with assistance, rather than waste money deciding who "deserves" help?**

2. Means-Testing vs. Universal Simplicity

A key reason UBI is often proposed as a **universal** program is because means-testing (determining who qualifies based on income or assets) is:

- **Expensive:**Requires significant government resources.
- **Inefficient:**People frequently fall through the cracks due to bureaucratic errors.
- **Unnecessary:** If UBI is funded by progressive taxation, wealthier individuals who receive it effectively return their payments through taxes.

With a **true UBI**, the administrative burden is significantly reduced because **every eligible person receives the payment without the need for application processes, oversight, or compliance checks.**

Do Conditional Programs Create Unnecessary Bureaucracy?

Beyond direct administrative costs, **conditional programs also create inefficiencies that harm recipients and the economy**.

1. The "Welfare Trap" and Work Disincentives

- Many conditional welfare programs unintentionally discourage work because **benefits are reduced or eliminated as income rises.**
- This creates a**welfare trap**, where individuals avoid higher-paying jobs or additional work hours to prevent losing benefits.

• A **no-strings-attached UBI** avoids this issue because **it does not disappear when someone earns more income.**

2. Complex Application Processes

• In the U.S., social programs like Medicaid, food assistance, and housing support require **lengthy applications, documentation, and interviews.**

• Many people who qualify for aid **never receive it** due to bureaucratic barriers.

• A universal, unconditional UBI would **eliminate paperwork and delays**, ensuring that support reaches everyone efficiently.

3. Fraud Prevention Costs vs. Simplicity

• Opponents of UBI worry about fraud, but fraud in cash-transfer programs is already **extremely low.**

• In the U.S., only about **1% of social program funds** are lost to fraud, yet governments spend billions enforcing compliance.

• A **universal** approach removes fraud incentives altogether—if everyone receives UBI, there's **no need to cheat the system.**

By **removing conditions**, governments can **reduce inefficiencies, lower costs, and ensure that benefits reach people without unnecessary barriers.**

How Might Restrictions Impact Recipients?

Placing conditions on UBI could create significant unintended consequences, making it **less effective** and **more harmful** for those who need it most.

1. Psychological Stress and Stigma

• Traditional welfare programs often come with **stigma**, leading recipients to feel **shame, anxiety, or embarrassment.**

• Conditional programs reinforce the idea that **only the "deserving poor" should receive aid**, which can be harmful to mental health and social well-being.

• A **no-strings-attached UBI** removes this stigma—since everyone gets it, there is **no shame in receiving it.**

2. Punitive Measures Can Hurt the Most Vulnerable

• Many welfare programs impose **work requirements**, but **not everyone can meet them** due to **disabilities, caregiving responsibilities, or lack of available jobs.**

• If UBI were conditional on employment, it could **exclude those who need financial security the most**.

• A true UBI would ensure **everyone has a financial floor, regardless of their employment status**.

3. Delays and Uncertainty Can Be Devastating

• Welfare recipients often experience **delays in payments** due to application backlogs, missing paperwork, or changes in eligibility.

• These delays can cause **evictions, food insecurity, and financial crises.**

• A no-strings-attached UBI would provide **consistent, predictable income**, allowing people to **plan ahead without fear of losing support**.

Conclusion: Why Unconditional UBI is the Most Efficient Model

The idea of **attaching conditions to UBI may seem reasonable on the surface**, but in practice, it **creates more problems than it solves. Conditional benefits require expensive bureaucracy, create inefficiencies, and often fail to reach those who need them most**.

A **no-strings-attached UBI eliminates these issues** by:

✓ **Reducing administrative costs**—no need for means-testing or compliance monitoring.

✓ **Ensuring that no one falls through the cracks**—everyone receives support, regardless of circumstances.

✓ **Encouraging work and entrepreneurship**—without the fear of losing benefits.

✓ **Providing dignity and security**—without unnecessary stigma or stress.

In short, a **universal and unconditional** UBI is not just about fairness—it's about **efficiency, effectiveness, and creating a stronger, more resilient society**.

We live in difference and that can make us strong. Policies are supported by some people and opposed by others. If we know why people oppose UBI, we can address those differences of opinion. By doing so, we can make the system work for everyone. The next chapter will focus on opposition to UBI.

CHAPTER 11
WHY SOME PEOPLE OPPOSE UBI

Introduction

While Universal Basic Income (UBI) has passionate supporters across the political and economic spectrum, it also faces significant opposition. Critics argue that **UBI is unrealistic, expensive, and potentially harmful to individual motivation and economic stability**. Opposition comes from various perspectives—some view it as a **threat to traditional work ethics**, while others believe it could **harm businesses and economic growth**. This chapter will explore the main arguments against UBI and why some people believe it is not the right solution.

Political and Ideological Objections

1. Opposition from Conservatives: Undermining Work Ethic

Many conservatives and right-leaning political groups oppose UBI because they believe **financial aid should be earned, not given unconditionally**. From this perspective:

- **Work is a moral value**— UBI could encourage laziness and reduce motivation to work.
- Government should focus on**creating jobs, not handing out money**.
- Welfare should be **targeted to those in genuine need**, not given universally.

2. Concerns from Progressives: Prioritizing Other Social Programs

Some progressives and left-leaning policymakers **do not oppose government assistance** but **question whether UBI is the best use of resources:**

- UBI might **divert funds from essential services**, such as **healthcare, education, and affordable housing**.
- Instead of giving everyone a fixed income, money might be better spent on **targeted social welfare programs** for the most vulnerable.
- UBI **does not address systemic issues** like rising housing costs, healthcare expenses, and wage stagnation.

3. Libertarian and Fiscal Conservative Concerns: Government Overreach

While some libertarians support UBI as a replacement for welfare, others **oppose it as an expansion of government power**:

- **Higher taxes** to fund UBI could give the government more control over private wealth.
- UBI could **increase long-term dependency on government aid**, reducing personal responsibility.
- Government programs are often **inefficient and expensive**, and UBI could become **another bureaucratic failure**.

Key Objection: Many ideological opponents worry that UBI would either discourage work, waste resources, or expand government influence in ways that are harmful to society.

Business and Economic Concerns

1. The Cost of UBI: Too Expensive to Sustain?

A major concern is that UBI could place **an unsustainable financial burden on governments**. Critics argue:

- UBI would require **massive increases in taxation**, either through higher income taxes, corporate taxes, or new levies like a **Value-Added Tax (VAT)**.
- Some fear that **higher taxes on businesses** could lead to **job losses, outsourcing, or reduced investment**.
- Government spending is already stretched in many countries—UBI could **compete with essential services** like healthcare, infrastructure, and education.

2. Inflation Concerns: Would Prices Rise?

Some economists worry that injecting large sums of money into the economy **could cause inflation**, meaning:

• If everyone has extra money,**businesses may raise prices**, canceling out the benefits of UBI.

• Housing, food, and other essential goods could become**more expensive**, making it harder for lower-income people to afford necessities.

• Countries with experiments in UBI (such as Alaska's oil dividend or Finland's UBI trial) **have not seen major inflation**, but critics argue that **a full-scale national UBI program could have different effects**.

3. Impact on the Labor Market

Opponents argue that UBI could disrupt the labor market by:

• **Reducing the incentive to work** leading to **labor shortages in key industries**.

• Making some jobs**unattractive**, forcing businesses to raise wages, which could drive up **consumer prices**.

• Encouraging people to **work less or leave the workforce entirely**, harming productivity and economic growth.

Key Objection: Business and economic critics worry that UBI is too expensive, could drive inflation, and might reduce overall workforce participation.

Fears of Dependency and Moral Hazard

1. Would UBI Encourage Laziness?

One of the strongest emotional arguments against UBI is the fear that **"free money" would make people lazy**. Critics claim:

• Work is **not just about money**—it provides structure, purpose, and social connection.

• Some people **may choose not to work at all**, relying only on UBI and contributing nothing back to society.

• Over time, a society that doesn't require work **could experience a decline in productivity and innovation**.

However, real-world UBI experiments **do not support this claim**—studies show that **most people continue working even when given unconditional income**.

2. The Slippery Slope: Expanding Dependency on Government

Some argue that UBI could create **a dangerous precedent**:

• Once people get used to receiving free money, they may **demand even more over time**.

• Future politicians could **increase UBI payments for votes**, leading to long-term economic instability.

• If people stop striving for economic self-sufficiency, **government could end up controlling more aspects of daily life**.

3. Social and Cultural Resistance

Many societies value **hard work and self-reliance**, and UBI challenges these beliefs. Opponents argue:

• People may look down on UBI recipients, seeing them as **"free riders"**.

• Some may resent having their **tax dollars used to support people who don't work**.

• If UBI replaces traditional work incentives, younger generations may **lose the motivation to build careers or contribute productively**.

Key Objection: Many opponents believe UBI undermines the value of work, creates dependency, and could weaken cultural attitudes toward self-sufficiency.

Conclusion: Is Opposition to UBI Justified?

The debate over UBI is complex. While critics raise valid concerns about **cost, economic disruption, and dependency**, supporters argue that **technological progress, automation, and inequality require new solutions**.

• **Some concerns, like work disincentives, are not strongly supported by evidence.**

• **Other concerns, like funding and inflation, require careful policy design to address.**

• **Public perception and cultural attitudes play a significant role in whether UBI would be widely accepted.**

As the conversation continues, the question is not just **whether UBI is a good idea, but how it could be structured to address these concerns**.

Next Chapter: How to Make UBI a Reality

If UBI is to be implemented, what steps need to be taken? The next chapter will explore **timelines, policy roadmaps, and political challenges** in making UBI a reality.

Next Chapter: How Do We Make UBI a Reality?

If UBI is necessary to prevent economic collapse, how can it be implemented? The next chapter will discuss **practical steps, political challenges, and realistic timelines for making UBI a reality**.

CHAPTER 12
WHO SUPPORTS UBI AND WHY?

Introduction

Universal Basic Income (UBI) has gained support from a wide range of individuals and groups, often for very different reasons. While some view it as a **safety net** for those displaced by automation, others see it as a way to **simplify government programs** or **promote economic freedom**. Interestingly, UBI has attracted advocates from across the political and economic spectrum, from **tech leaders** to **social progressives** to **libertarians**.

This chapter will explore why these diverse groups support UBI, their motivations, and how their perspectives shape different policy proposals.

Tech Leaders and Automation Advocates

One of the most vocal groups supporting UBI consists of **tech industry leaders**, many of whom see automation and artificial intelligence as **revolutionizing the workforce and making traditional jobs obsolete**. These advocates argue that as machines take over more tasks, society must ensure that people still have **income, purchasing power, and financial security**.

1. The Automation Argument

- Advancements in **robotics, AI, and machine learning** are reducing the need for human labor across various industries.

• Jobs in **manufacturing, transportation, retail, and even white-collar sectors** are at risk of disappearing.

• Without an income replacement system, job displacement could lead to **mass unemployment, economic instability, and social unrest.**

2. UBI as a Safety Net for Job Displacement

• Tech leaders like **Elon Musk, Mark Zuckerberg, and Sam Altman** have argued that **as automation eliminates jobs, UBI will be necessary to keep the economy running.**

• A guaranteed income would allow displaced workers to **retrain for new careers**, pursue entrepreneurship, or **contribute to society in non-traditional ways.**

• Without UBI, growing **income inequality** could create a **two-tiered society**—one where only the wealthy benefit from automation while millions struggle to survive.

3. Supporting Innovation and Consumer Demand

• If people lose their jobs to automation and **don't have an income**, they won't be able to **spend money on goods and services**, which could **hurt businesses.**

• UBI ensures **continued consumer demand**, helping businesses **thrive in an increasingly automated world.**

• By providing financial security, UBI **frees individuals to take risks**, launch startups, and explore creative or entrepreneurial ventures.

Key Perspective:

Tech industry leaders support UBI **as a long-term solution** to automation-driven unemployment and **to ensure economic stability in a world where machines do most of the work.**

Economists and Social Progressives

Many **economists and social progressives** support UBI **as a tool to reduce poverty, increase economic mobility, and promote human dignity.** This group sees UBI as **a way to address structural inequality** and **modernize social welfare systems.**

1. Reducing Poverty and Income Inequality

• Traditional welfare programs are often **complex, bureaucratic, and insufficient.**

• UBI **ensures a basic level of financial security for everyone**, reducing reliance on **food stamps, unemployment benefits, and other fragmented programs**.

• Countries that have tested UBI-like programs (such as Finland and Canada) found that it **helped lift people out of poverty without discouraging work**.

2. Empowering Workers and Strengthening Labor Markets

• UBI gives workers more bargaining power by**allowing them to refuse exploitative jobs**.

• Without the desperation of needing any job to survive, people can **demand fair wages and better working conditions**.

• This could reduce reliance on**predatory employers**, improve job quality, and even lead to shorter workweeks.

3. Investing in Human Potential

• Many people are stuck in**dead-end jobs simply to survive**, preventing them from pursuing **education, caregiving, or entrepreneurship**.

• UBI would allow individuals to**return to school, learn new skills, and explore creative or productive passions**.

• With financial security, people could contribute to society in**non-traditional ways**, such as **volunteering, caregiving, or starting new community projects**.

4. Economic Stimulus and Growth

• When people at the bottom of the income scale receive extra money, they **spend it on essentials like food, housing, and healthcare**, boosting the local economy.

• Studies have shown that direct cash transfers lead to**higher economic activity and business growth**, benefiting society as a whole.

Key Perspective:

Economists and social progressives support UBI **as a poverty-fighting tool, a way to empower workers, and an investment in human potential.**

Libertarians and the Idea of a Streamlined Government

Interestingly, many **libertarians**—who typically favor smaller government and fewer social programs—also **support UBI**, though for very different reasons. They see UBI as a **simpler, more efficient alternative to the current welfare system**.

1. Replacing the Welfare State with Direct Cash Payments

• Many libertarians argue that **the existing welfare system is inefficient and riddled with bureaucracy**.

• Instead of maintaining **hundreds of overlapping programs** (food stamps, housing assistance, unemployment benefits, etc.), a single **UBI payment could replace them all**.

• This would **reduce government waste, cut administrative costs, and give people more control over how they spend their money**.

2. Promoting Individual Freedom and Responsibility

• Unlike traditional welfare, which comes with **rules and restrictions**, UBI **allows individuals to make their own financial decisions**.

• Recipients wouldn't be required to prove they are job-seeking, attending training programs, or meeting work requirements.

• **People would have the freedom to use their money however they see fit**, whether for education, starting a business, or taking care of family.

3. Encouraging Market-Based Solutions

• UBI shifts power **away from government-run assistance programs** and puts it **directly into the hands of individuals**.

• Instead of government deciding **who gets assistance and how it is spent**, individuals would have the flexibility to **spend money based on their unique needs**.

• This fits with the libertarian belief that **people, not bureaucracies, are best suited to determine their own well-being**.

4. Potential to Reduce Government Dependency

• While some critics fear UBI would increase reliance on government, libertarians argue that **it would actually do the opposite**.

• Many welfare recipients are trapped in **complex programs that discourage work**, but **UBI removes disincentives** and lets individuals take control of their finances.

• If structured properly, UBI could actually **reduce long-term dependency on government programs**.

Key Perspective:

Libertarians support UBI **as a means of reducing government bureaucracy, promoting individual freedom, and replacing inefficient welfare programs with a simple cash payment**.

Conclusion: A Diverse Coalition for UBI

While UBI has its critics, it also enjoys **broad support from different political and economic perspectives**.

- **Tech leaders** see UBI as a way to **address automation-driven job loss** and keep the economy stable.
- **Economists and social progressives** view UBI as **a tool to fight poverty, increase economic mobility, and empower workers**.
- **Libertarians** support UBI as a means of **reducing government bureaucracy and promoting economic freedom**.

Despite their **different motivations**, these groups share a common belief: **UBI could be a transformative policy for the future**. The challenge is in **designing a system that balances affordability, effectiveness, and political feasibility**.

As the conditions for living transform, problems arise, that did not exist before. If we have some idea of what happens if we don't act, it's more possible to understand the importance of change. This will give us more confidence to take action that has not been done before, but is necessary because the conditions of life have changed. The next chapter will explore what happens if we do nothing.

CHAPTER 13
WHAT HAPPENS IF NOTHING IS DONE?

Introduction

Universal Basic Income (UBI) is often debated as a **potential solution** to economic instability, job loss due to automation, and rising inequality. However, what if UBI is never implemented? What happens if governments do nothing in response to these major economic shifts?

This chapter explores the potential consequences of **inaction**, including the long-term effects of automation on employment, growing wealth disparities, and the risk of social unrest. We will also examine potential future economic scenarios if no proactive measures are taken.

The Impact of Automation on Jobs

1. The Rise of AI and Robotics

Technological advancements in artificial intelligence, robotics, and machine learning are transforming industries at an **unprecedented rate**. Many jobs that once required human labor are now being **automated** or **augmented by technology**, including:

- **Manufacturing:** Factory jobs have already seen massive automation, replacing assembly line workers with robots.
- **Retail & Customer Service:** Self-checkout kiosks and AI-powered chatbots are reducing the need for cashiers and customer service representatives.

- **Transportation:** Self-driving technology threatens millions of jobs in trucking, delivery services, and taxi driving.
- **Finance & Legal Work:**AI-driven software can now **analyze contracts, process transactions, and make investment decisions**, reducing the demand for lawyers, accountants, and financial analysts.

2. The Speed of Job Displacement

Unlike past industrial revolutions, **modern automation is accelerating at a faster pace**. Previous technological advancements created **new industries and jobs**, but today's automation does not guarantee the same level of replacement.

- **Fewer new jobs are being created**compared to those being lost.
- Many of the jobs created by technology require **specialized skills**, leaving behind workers who lack technical education.
- Low-skilled workers may **struggle to transition** to new industries, leading to long-term unemployment.

If governments do nothing, **millions of people could find themselves permanently unemployed** with no safety net.

3. The Shrinking Middle Class

- The automation of middle-class jobs **widens the gap between the wealthy and the poor**.
- Wealth is concentrated in the hands of those who own automation technologies, leaving displaced workers struggling to survive.
- Without intervention, automation could **hollow out the middle class**, leading to **economic stagnation and declining consumer spending**.

Key Consequence: Without UBI or another form of economic restructuring, automation could leave millions of workers **without income, job security, or a path to financial stability**.

Rising Inequality and Social Unrest

1. Widening the Wealth Gap

Inaction in the face of automation and economic transformation will likely lead to:

- **More billionaires and corporate monopolies** as technology replaces human labor and increases productivity without raising wages.
- **Stagnant or declining wages** for workers who cannot transition into high-paying tech jobs.

- **Weakened bargaining power** for employees as job competition increases, leading to **worse working conditions.**

The economic divide between **those who own technology** and **those who rely on wages** will widen, creating **deepening inequality.**

2. Increased Poverty and Homelessness

With fewer well-paying jobs available and **rising costs of living**, more people may:

- Struggle to afford housing, healthcare, andeducation.
- Become **dependent on welfare programs**, stretching government budgets.
- Experience**housing insecurity**, leading to increased homelessness.

Governments that **fail to address economic displacement** may face **an overwhelmed social safety net**, making it harder to provide assistance to those in need.

3. Social Unrest and Political Instability

Economic inequality **has historically been linked to social unrest**. If people feel they have no economic opportunities, they may:

- **Lose trust in governments** leading to political instability.
- Engage in**protests, strikes, or even violent demonstrations.**
- Support **extremist political movements**, blaming specific groups for economic hardship.

Historical examples—such as the Great Depression and the 2008 financial crisis—show that **widespread economic distress can lead to political turmoil and civil unrest.**

Key Consequence: If nothing is done, societies could face **rising poverty, political instability, and increasing hostility toward governments and corporations.**

Future Economic Scenarios

1. The "Winner-Takes-All" Economy

Without UBI or an alternative system to distribute wealth, the future economy could be **dominated by a few wealthy elites**, while most of the population struggles to get by.

- **AI-driven corporations** will increase productivity but may employ **fewer workers.**

• Governments that fail to implement redistributive policies may see **declining consumer demand**, hurting economic growth.

• The economy could shift into **a permanent recession** due to lack of consumer spending power.

2. A Two-Tiered Society

A world without intervention could create **two economic classes**:

1 **The elite class** A small percentage of people who own businesses, automation, and intellectual property—controlling the majority of wealth.

2 **The struggling majority** People unable to find stable employment, relying on a **patchwork of part-time work, gig jobs, and government assistance**.

Without a financial buffer like UBI, **economic security would become a privilege, not a right**.

3. The Rise of Radical Economic Solutions

If governments fail to act, **public pressure for drastic measures will grow**, potentially leading to:

• **Forced wealth redistribution** through higher taxation or corporate regulation.

• **Massive expansion of welfare programs** straining public budgets.

• **Nationalization of industries** to prevent monopolies from controlling economic output.

These measures could have **unintended consequences**, such as **driving businesses and investments away**, creating **economic stagnation or even collapse**.

Key Consequence: If policymakers ignore economic displacement, the **eventual solutions may be radical, disruptive, and potentially harmful to economic stability**.

Conclusion: Why Action is Necessary

Failing to address **automation, economic inequality, and labor displacement** will not only **harm individuals but also destabilize entire economies and societies**. The consequences of inaction could include:

• **Mass unemployment and job insecurity** due to automation.

• **Growing economic inequality** leading to unrest and political instability.

• **A weaker, less resilient economy** as fewer people have the financial means to contribute.

UBI as a Preventative Measure

While UBI is not the only solution, it is **one of the most direct ways** to address the consequences of automation and rising inequality. By providing **a financial safety net**, UBI could:

- **Prevent mass poverty**by ensuring everyone has basic income security.
- **Stimulate the economy**by keeping consumer demand high.
- **Reduce social unrest**by creating a more stable and equitable society.

Next Chapter: The Timeline for Making UBI Happen

Now that we've explored the public's willingness to pay for UBI, how can it become a reality? The next chapter will outline a **step-by-step timeline** for implementing UBI, covering short-term pilot programs, gradual expansion, and full-scale implementation.

CHAPTER 14
A TIMELINE FOR MAKING UBI HAPPEN

Introduction

The concept of Universal Basic Income (UBI) has garnered increasing attention in recent years, with governments, tech leaders, and activists recognizing its potential to address economic insecurity, rising inequality, and the impacts of automation. Yet, while the idea holds promise, implementing UBI is no simple task. It requires **strategic planning**, **incremental implementation**, and overcoming significant **political and logistical hurdles**.

In this chapter, we explore how UBI could be brought into reality. We will outline **steps for pilot programs**, discuss how to **scale UBI** to reach broader populations, and examine the **political and legislative challenges** that must be overcome for UBI to become a sustainable policy.

Steps for Pilot Programs and Gradual Implementation

1. The Need for Pilot Programs

Before embarking on full-scale implementation, it's crucial to **test the viability of UBI** through pilot programs. These programs would allow policymakers to gauge the **effectiveness, costs**, and **impact** of UBI in different populations and regions. The lessons learned from pilot programs will provide essential data to fine-tune the program's structure and **address potential challenges**.

- **Small-Scale Trials:** Start with **local or regional pilots** that provide a basic income to a selected group of people. Cities or states with a history of progressive policies may be more inclined to adopt UBI pilot programs.
- **Varying Demographics:** The pilots should include **diverse demographics** to assess how UBI impacts various age groups, employment statuses, and socio-economic backgrounds.
- **Funding Sources:** These programs should explore how UBI can be funded from a variety of sources, such as **carbon taxes, wealth taxes**, or **redistribution of welfare funds**.
- **Duration and Data Collection:** Pilot programs should run for **at least 12 to 24 months** to provide sufficient time for meaningful data collection and analysis. The data will inform the policy's **sustainability, behavioral impact**, and the **economic repercussions** of a wider rollout.

2. Scaling Up: From Pilot to National Rollout

Once pilot programs have provided critical insights into how UBI works in practice, the next step is to **gradually scale up**. This step will likely be complex and require a phased approach to ensure that the system is manageable and economically sustainable.

- **Gradual Expansion:** Begin by expanding UBI eligibility to additional **income brackets** and gradually move from local/regional programs to **state or national programs**. For instance, a city-based pilot could expand to a state, then to a federal rollout.
- **Increasing Benefit Amounts:** Start with a **partial basic income**—a lower amount that covers essential needs—and gradually increase it to the full amount as economic conditions allow.
- **Integrating with Existing Welfare Systems:**As UBI is scaled up, it can be integrated with existing welfare programs, either by **phasing out or consolidating** other forms of assistance (e.g., food stamps, unemployment benefits). This would minimize redundancies and ensure a **smooth transition**.
- **Sustainable Funding** By gradually increasing the tax base, UBI can be funded by implementing **progressive tax systems** (wealth taxes, VAT, or carbon taxes). As the program scales, more revenue sources will be needed to ensure sustainability.

Policy Transitions and Scaling Up

1. Policy Reforms and Adjustments

When moving from pilot programs to a broader rollout, the implementation of **policy reforms** becomes essential. These adjustments will help ensure that the UBI system aligns with broader economic and social objectives, such as reducing inequality and fostering financial security.

- **Tax Reforms:** A substantial **tax overhaul** is necessary to ensure that there is adequate funding for UBI. Progressive taxation on the **wealthiest individuals, corporations**, and **environmental impact taxes** (such as a carbon tax) could help offset the costs.
- **Reforming the Welfare State:** Moving toward UBI may require **restructuring current welfare programs**. This could mean consolidating various forms of assistance into a single payment that can be delivered to individuals without bureaucratic complexity.
- **Labor Market Policies:** As UBI implementation progresses, **labor market policies** may also need to be adjusted. This includes transitioning away from traditional welfare-to-work programs, replacing them with **more flexible work opportunities** for those who still want to participate in the workforce.

2. Addressing Regional Differences

A phased implementation of UBI would also require policymakers to account for **regional disparities**. Differences in the cost of living between rural and urban areas, for example, may require varying benefit amounts to ensure equity.

- **Tailored Benefits:** Policymakers could introduce **regional benefit rates**, adjusting UBI amounts to reflect **local economic realities**. This could include larger amounts for high-cost areas (e.g., cities) and smaller amounts for rural areas, without diminishing the core purpose of UBI.

3. Infrastructure and Administrative Systems

A national rollout of UBI would demand significant **investment in infrastructure**. This includes the creation of **administrative systems** capable of processing millions of payments. Modernized digital platforms, bank account integrations, and **identity verification** systems would ensure **smooth delivery**.

- **Digital Delivery:** UBI could be administered through **direct deposits**, similar to stimulus checks or social security payments, making it simple and transparent for recipients to access.
- **Preventing Fraud:** Ensuring that UBI payments are distributed accu-

rately and without fraud would require robust **digital systems** with **anti-fraud measures**, including ID checks and authentication processes.

Political and Legislative Challenges

1. Political Resistance

The largest obstacle to implementing UBI is **political resistance**. Although UBI has **gained traction among tech leaders, economists, and social progressives**, it faces strong opposition from various political ideologies and special interest groups.

- **Conservative Opposition:** Conservatives often argue that UBI represents an unsustainable **entitlement program**, fearing that it would lead to **higher taxes, increased government spending**, and **dependency**.
- **Progressive Concerns:** Some progressives might argue that UBI is insufficient on its own and could **divert attention away from structural reforms** like **healthcare, education**, or **housing**.
- **Corporate Interests:** Businesses that benefit from cheap labor (e.g., fast food chains, gig economy companies) may resist UBI, fearing that it could **increase labor costs** and reduce their profit margins.

2. Coalition Building and Political Will

To overcome political resistance, UBI proponents must build **broad coalitions**. This requires framing UBI as a **bipartisan solution** that addresses economic issues such as automation, job displacement, and inequality, while ensuring it remains fiscally sustainable.

- **Cross-party Advocacy:** Attracting advocates from both the left and the right will be crucial. For example, libertarians may support UBI because it simplifies welfare programs and reduces government bureaucracy, while progressives may champion it as a tool for addressing economic inequality.
- **Mobilizing Public Support:** A key to overcoming political resistance will be **public education** campaigns to help voters understand the benefits of UBI, including the potential for reducing poverty and stimulating local economies.

3. Legislative Process

For UBI to become a reality, it must pass through **legislative hurdles**. This involves **drafting laws**, holding **committee hearings**, and **securing votes** in both the House and Senate.

- **Public Pressure:** Strong public support could help sway legislators to prioritize UBI. Advocacy campaigns and grassroots movements will be essential to ensuring that UBI remains a top political issue.

- **Negotiation and Compromise:**Expect compromises along the way, such as **scaled-back versions** of UBI or pilot programs that gradually transition into full-scale implementation.

Conclusion

Implementing Universal Basic Income is no easy feat, but a **gradual, phased approach** can make it more manageable. By starting with **pilot programs**, ensuring effective **policy transitions**, and overcoming **political resistance**, UBI could become a cornerstone of future economic systems. Although there are **significant legislative and political challenges**, the growing evidence for UBI's potential benefits—along with the urgency of addressing automation, inequality, and job displacement—makes it a pressing issue that cannot be ignored.

Next Chapter: Are Vouchers a Better Alternative to Cash?

Some critics argue that instead of cash, a UBI should come in the form of **vouchers for housing, food, or healthcare**. But do vouchers provide the same flexibility and dignity as cash? The next chapter will explore whether **restricted spending programs** are a viable alternative to a **no-strings-attached UBI**.

CHAPTER 15
ARE VOUCHERS BETTER THAN CASH?

Introduction

The question of whether **vouchers** or **cash** is a more effective method of providing assistance has long been debated. Vouchers are often seen as a way to **target assistance** to specific needs, while cash provides the recipient with the freedom to choose how to spend it. With Universal Basic Income (UBI) at the center of discussions about economic security, this chapter explores the merits and drawbacks of both systems, comparing them in terms of **effectiveness**, **flexibility**, and **efficiency**.

By examining the **history of targeted assistance programs** and learning from past welfare models, we can better understand the strengths and weaknesses of vouchers versus cash and how UBI fits into this broader conversation.

The Case for Targeted Assistance: Why Vouchers?

1. Addressing Specific Needs

Vouchers are often viewed as a way to ensure that assistance is used for its intended purpose. For example, **food stamps** or **housing vouchers** provide recipients with specific benefits that can only be used for food or housing-related expenses, preventing misuse of funds. Proponents of this approach argue that vouchers:

- **Guarantee the proper allocation**of resources: By restricting how benefits are spent, vouchers can ensure that funds go directly to **basic needs**, such as food, shelter, or healthcare.
- **Prevent wasteful spending** Critics of cash assistance argue that individuals may spend cash on non-essential or harmful goods, like cigarettes or alcohol. Vouchers mitigate this risk by limiting spending to specific categories.
- **Support policy goals** Vouchers can be targeted to specific groups or goals, such as **food insecurity**, **low-income housing**, or **childcare**, ensuring that public funds are focused where they are most needed.

2. Ensuring Equity

Vouchers can also be seen as a tool for achieving greater **equity**. When distributing resources, governments can design voucher programs that address **disparities in need**. For instance, a food assistance program may give higher-value vouchers to households with more children or individuals facing more severe economic hardship. This creates a system of **progressive assistance**, where those in greater need receive more help.

Moreover, vouchers can be tailored to local economic conditions. For example, a **housing voucher** program might provide different subsidy amounts depending on the local housing market, ensuring that the assistance meets the cost of living in a given area.

3. Targeting for Cost-Efficiency

Another argument in favor of vouchers is their potential for **cost-effectiveness**. Because vouchers target specific needs, they can reduce the risk of **overspending** or **misallocation of funds**. For instance, by limiting the areas in which funds can be used, governments can maximize the **value per dollar** spent and direct resources where they will have the greatest impact.

Why Some Argue Cash is More Effective

1. Flexibility and Autonomy

Cash, in contrast to vouchers, provides the **recipient with autonomy**. People can choose how to spend the money according to their unique circumstances, rather than being restricted to certain categories of goods or services. Proponents of cash assistance argue that:

- **Personalized Needs** People have different priorities, and cash allows them to meet their needs in a **way that suits their personal situation**. For example, some individuals may need help paying for rent, while others might prioritize healthcare or transportation costs. Cash assistance enables recipients to **make decisions** about their lives and finances.

- **Simplicity and Efficiency** Cash transfers are often easier to administer than voucher programs. There are no complex rules to follow, and recipients don't need to navigate multiple systems or paperwork to redeem benefits. This **streamlines the process**, reducing administrative costs and delays.

2. Reducing Stigma and Dignity

Cash assistance tends to carry less **stigma** than vouchers. Vouchers often signal that the recipient is **dependent** on the government for specific services, and recipients may face **embarrassment** when using them in public. With cash, recipients have more **freedom** and **dignity** in their spending choices, potentially leading to greater **social acceptance** of the assistance.

Moreover, cash payments do not set people apart as much as vouchers do, reducing the social stigma associated with receiving help. In a society where financial insecurity is already a source of stress and alienation, cash can serve as a tool to **empower** individuals rather than label them as dependent on government aid.

3. Behavioral Impact

The flexibility of cash can also have positive **psychological impacts**. By receiving cash, individuals may feel more **empowered** to make long-term financial decisions and plan for their futures. The **autonomy** to prioritize different aspects of their lives (whether that's paying off debt, investing in education, or saving for emergencies) can help recipients feel more **in control** of their economic situation.

Lessons from Past Welfare Programs

1. The Failures of Targeted Assistance

Many targeted welfare programs, such as **food stamps** and **housing subsidies**, have faced **criticism** for being too complex, inefficient, or stigmatizing. While these programs aim to address specific needs, they often fail to adequately meet the needs of all recipients:

- **Complexity and Overhead** Targeted programs often require a **complicated application process**, eligibility criteria, and administrative systems, which can lead to delays, errors, and inefficiencies. This increases the cost of delivery and can discourage individuals from seeking assistance.
- **Overlapping Programs** Many targeted assistance programs overlap in

their goals, creating redundancy and confusion. A person may qualify for **food assistance**, but not for **housing subsidies**, or vice versa, leaving them vulnerable in areas not covered by existing programs. This fragmentation can fail to address the broader, interconnected nature of poverty.

- **Exclusion and Eligibility Gaps** Despite their intent, targeted programs often fail to provide adequate assistance to those who fall just outside of the eligibility thresholds, or those who may need help but aren't covered by a specific program. Cash transfers, on the other hand, leave no one behind who meets the eligibility criteria.

2. UBI and Lessons Learned

Universal Basic Income (UBI) aims to **overcome many of these limitations** by offering a **simpler, more inclusive solution**. Unlike targeted programs, UBI is **unconditional**, providing everyone who qualifies with the same benefit, regardless of their specific needs. This reduces the **administrative burden** and ensures that no one falls through the cracks due to complex eligibility rules.

Moreover, UBI removes the **stigma** that often accompanies welfare programs, as everyone receives the same amount of assistance, regardless of their circumstances. By focusing on **cash rather than vouchers**, UBI embraces the principles of **autonomy, simplicity**, and **dignity**, ensuring that recipients can decide for themselves how best to use the funds.

Conclusion

The question of whether **vouchers** or **cash** is the better method of assistance is complex and depends on a variety of factors, including the goals of the assistance program, the needs of recipients, and the broader economic context. Vouchers can be more targeted and efficient in ensuring that benefits are used for specific needs, but they also come with the challenges of **administrative complexity** and **limited flexibility**.

Cash, on the other hand, provides recipients with **freedom of choice**, reduces stigma, and is simpler to administer. While cash may not always address specific needs as directly as vouchers, its flexibility and ability to empower recipients make it a powerful tool for promoting financial security.

As we look to the future, **Universal Basic Income** represents an attempt to combine the best aspects of both systems. By providing **unconditional cash payments**, UBI could **simplify welfare**, reduce bureaucratic hurdles, and give individuals the ability to make their own decisions about how to best use the resources available to them. Through lessons learned from past welfare programs and the ongoing debate between vouchers and cash, we can better understand how to move forward in addressing the needs of those most vulnerable in society.

In the next chapter, we will explore how **UBI can coexist with other progressive economic policies** and what the future of work might look like in a world where financial security is guaranteed for all.

Can a UBI help people with drug problems, mental illness, and people who get out of prison? The next chapter will focus on these issues.

CHAPTER 16
UNIVERSAL BASIC INCOME—A LIFELINE FOR THE FORGOTTEN

Introduction

In a society driven by ruthless economic forces, many individuals fall through the cracks, unable to secure a stable existence due to factors beyond their control. Among the most vulnerable are people struggling with drug addiction, those with mental health challenges, and former convicts reentering society. These groups often find themselves in a vicious cycle of poverty, instability, and societal neglect. Universal Basic Income (UBI) offers a transformative solution—providing a financial foundation that enables them to regain control of their lives, reduce stress, and reintegrate into society as productive, stable individuals.

1. Helping People Struggling with Addiction

Addiction is often both a cause and a consequence of economic hardship. Many individuals turn to drugs as a means of coping with trauma, stress, and the despair of poverty. Once addicted, their struggle intensifies as they face employment discrimination, legal troubles, and the difficulty of affording rehabilitation services.

A UBI could serve as a crucial intervention in breaking this cycle. By ensuring a guaranteed income, it reduces the financial desperation that often drives people toward crime or dangerous behaviors to sustain their addiction. It also provides the stability necessary for long-term recovery, enabling individuals to seek treatment without the fear of financial ruin. Countries that have experimented with cash transfer programs have found that when people's basic needs are met, drug and alcohol consumption actually decreases because economic stability reduces stress and despair—the key drivers of substance abuse.

Furthermore, addiction treatment programs are expensive, and many people drop out due to financial pressure. With a UBI, they would have the means to complete rehabilitation without the looming threat of homelessness or starvation. Instead of punishing addiction through criminalization, society can address its root causes by ensuring people have enough money to live with dignity.

2. Supporting Those with Mental Health Challenges

Mental illness affects millions, yet it remains one of the most neglected issues in economic policy. Many people suffering from depression, anxiety, bipolar disorder, or schizophrenia are unable to work consistently, making them highly vulnerable to financial instability. Without money for housing, medication, or therapy, they often end up homeless or institutionalized, cycling in and out of emergency rooms and jails.

A UBI would be life-changing for those with mental health challenges. It would ensure that they can afford stable housing, food, and medication, removing the financial stress that often exacerbates their conditions. Studies show that poverty and financial insecurity are significant triggers for mental illness, and reducing these stressors can lead to improved mental health outcomes.

Additionally, people with mental illnesses often struggle to navigate the complex bureaucracy of disability benefits. A UBI, being unconditional, would eliminate this burden, providing a simple, reliable financial safety net without requiring people to prove their incapacity over and over again. This shift from a punitive, conditional welfare system to an empowering, unconditional income would allow individuals to focus on treatment and personal development rather than mere survival.

3. Giving Former Convicts a Second Chance

For those leaving prison, reintegration into society is an uphill battle. Employers are reluctant to hire individuals with criminal records, housing is difficult to obtain, and many former inmates lack the skills or support needed to rebuild their lives. As a result, recidivism rates are high—many people return to crime out of sheer economic necessity.

A UBI would provide former convicts with the financial foundation necessary to start anew. By guaranteeing a basic level of income, it would reduce the desperation that often drives people back into illegal activities. Instead of being released into a world that has effectively abandoned them, former inmates would have a fair shot at reintegration.

Moreover, a UBI could complement rehabilitation programs by offering a financial cushion that allows individuals to pursue education, job training, or entrepreneurial ventures. It would give them the opportunity to develop a lawful and productive livelihood rather than being trapped in a cycle of unemployment and poverty. Studies have shown that economic stability is one of the most important factors in preventing recidivism. By providing that stability upfront, society can reduce crime rates and lower the enormous costs of mass incarceration.

Conclusion

Universal Basic Income is not just a policy for economic justice—it is a necessity for social stability and human dignity. For drug addicts seeking recovery, people with mental health challenges striving for stability, and former convicts trying to rebuild their lives, UBI could mean the difference between suffering and survival, between exclusion and inclusion.

Rather than punishing those who struggle, society must recognize that economic hardship often lies at the root of these problems. By ensuring that every person has enough money to meet their basic needs, we can reduce suffering, unlock human potential, and build a more compassionate, functioning society. UBI is not a handout—it is an investment in people, their well-being, and the collective future of our communities.

A UBI will add a significant amount of spending power, which can generate an increase use of fossil fuels, which could make climate change worse or could it be set up to reduce climate change? The next chapter will focus on this issue.

CHAPTER 17
UNIVERSAL BASIC INCOME AND ITS IMPACT ON CLIMATE CHANGE

Introduction

Universal Basic Income (UBI) is often discussed in terms of economic security, social justice, and poverty reduction, but its relationship with climate change is equally significant. The concern is twofold: If people receive a guaranteed income, will they spend more and increase consumption, thus exacerbating climate change? Or, could a UBI actually reduce emissions by shifting consumption patterns, decreasing reliance on environmentally harmful government services, and enabling people to make sustainable choices?

This chapter explores the environmental implications of UBI, examining both the risks and potential benefits. While critics argue that UBI could drive overconsumption, a well-designed system could instead promote sustainability by changing how and where people spend their money, reducing economic desperation, and enabling a transition to a greener economy.

1. Will More Money Mean More Consumption and Pollution?

One of the primary concerns about UBI is that giving people more financial security will lead to an increase in consumption, which in turn drives up production, energy use, and carbon emissions. Historically, as incomes rise, so does the demand for goods and services, many of which have a large environmental footprint. For example, increased spending on cars, electronics, and meat-based diets could lead to higher greenhouse gas emissions.

However, the relationship between income and environmental impact is not straightforward. Studies show that wealthier populations tend to spend more on services rather than material goods. A UBI, rather than leading to unchecked consumption, may shift spending toward education, healthcare, and leisure activities that have lower carbon footprints compared to mass consumption of physical goods.

Additionally, when people are less financially desperate, they may make more sustainable choices. For example, someone with a stable income might opt for a slightly more expensive but longer-lasting product rather than cheap, disposable alternatives. They may also be able to afford local, organic food instead of relying on mass-produced, carbon-intensive options. A UBI could thus promote a culture of mindful consumption rather than excess waste.

2. Reducing Reliance on High-Carbon Government Services

Paradoxically, when people lack money, they often rely on government services that are themselves environmentally costly. Many government programs are structured around mass-scale, high-energy consumption models, from large-scale food assistance programs that rely on industrial agriculture to subsidized housing developments that prioritize cost over sustainability.

For example:

- **Public Assistance and Industrial Agriculture:** Food stamp programs, while essential, often support large agribusinesses that are major polluters. A UBI, by giving people direct purchasing power, could allow them to buy from local farmers and sustainable food sources rather than relying on government-supported mass food distribution.
- **Emergency Services and Homelessness:** When people are homeless or in extreme poverty, they rely on emergency shelters, hospitals, and policing, all of which are expensive and energy-intensive. A UBI could reduce these costs by providing the stability needed to avoid emergency interventions.
- **Public Transportation vs. Car Dependency:** While public transit is often seen as a climate solution, many low-income areas lack efficient options, forcing people into high-emission vehicles. A UBI might enable people to relocate to areas with better infrastructure, reducing reliance on long commutes.

By alleviating poverty directly, UBI could reduce dependence on these large, carbon-intensive government programs, leading to a more efficient allocation of resources.

3. Enabling Sustainable Lifestyles

A key argument for UBI's environmental benefits is that financial security allows people to make long-term, sustainable choices rather than short-term survival-based decisions. Many people in poverty rely on cheap, unsustainable products because they have no other option. Fast fashion, processed food, and low-quality appliances all contribute to climate change, yet these are often the only affordable choices for those living paycheck to paycheck.

With a UBI, people would have the financial breathing room to make better choices:

- **Buying Durable Goods Instead of Cheap, Disposable Ones:** A stable income could allow consumers to invest in quality products that last longer, reducing waste.
- **Choosing Sustainable Housing:** Instead of being forced into substandard housing with poor insulation and high energy costs, UBI recipients could move into more efficient homes, reducing their carbon footprint.
- **Supporting Green Jobs and Local Economies:** A UBI could enable more people to pursue careers in sustainable industries, such as renewable energy, regenerative agriculture, and repair-based businesses rather than being forced into whatever job pays the bills.

4. Decoupling Work from Carbon-Intensive Industries

One of the biggest environmental benefits of UBI is that it could allow people to leave carbon-intensive jobs and transition to greener sectors. Many industries that contribute to climate change—such as fossil fuel extraction, deforestation, and factory farming—offer some of the few employment opportunities available to those in financial distress.

With a guaranteed income, workers would have greater flexibility to seek employment in sustainable industries, start their own eco-friendly businesses, or even participate in community-based initiatives like urban farming and renewable energy cooperatives. The current system forces many people to take whatever job they can find, regardless of its environmental impact. A UBI could help break this cycle.

Conclusion

The impact of Universal Basic Income on climate change is complex but largely positive when designed and implemented with sustainability in mind. While increased financial security can lead to higher consumption, it can also shift spending patterns toward more sustainable goods and services. More importantly, UBI could reduce dependence on environmentally harmful government programs, enable people to make greener choices, and support a transition away from carbon-intensive industries.

Rather than seeing UBI as a threat to the environment, we should recognize its potential as a tool for climate resilience. By lifting people out of poverty and giving them the freedom to make sustainable decisions, UBI can help create a society where both people and the planet can thrive.

A UBI on a scale as big as the United States has never been done before. How can smooth transitions and adjusting of the main variables improve the chance of success? The next chapter will explore these issues.

CHAPTER 18
CONCLUSION: THE FUTURE OF UNIVERSAL BASIC INCOME

Introduction

The concept of **Universal Basic Income (UBI)** is no longer a fringe idea or utopian fantasy; it has firmly entered the mainstream conversation about the future of work, poverty, and social security. What was once a controversial and experimental policy is gaining increasing attention from policymakers, economists, and social advocates around the world.

But as we stand at the crossroads of economic change, technological disruption, and rising inequality, the question remains: will **UBI become inevitable?** In this concluding chapter, we'll explore the future of UBI through the lens of **historical lessons**, **modern experiments**, and the **next steps** in the global movement toward a more equitable society.

Will UBI Become Inevitable?

A Growing Consensus on Economic Challenges

The world is witnessing rapid economic shifts that are redefining the very structure of labor markets and social safety nets. The rise of **automation**, **artificial intelligence**, and **globalization** has brought about massive changes in employment, with millions of jobs at risk of being displaced by technology. Meanwhile, the inequality gap continues to widen, with a growing divide between the wealthy and those struggling to make ends meet.

At the same time, governments are grappling with the increasing pressure on social welfare systems. Current safety nets are often inadequate, fragmented, and difficult to navigate, leaving many vulnerable people with no support. UBI presents a **unified solution**—a direct, unconditional income to ensure basic financial security for all citizens, regardless of employment status or income.

In many ways, UBI is rapidly becoming a **logical** and **necessary response** to these converging issues. As automation reduces the availability of traditional jobs, UBI could serve as a financial cushion for those left behind, offering a safety net in an economy that may no longer be able to provide employment for everyone. If UBI becomes a cornerstone of future policy, it may indeed become **inevitable**—an essential tool for preserving social stability in a changing world.

Political Will and Global Trends

However, the inevitability of UBI will depend largely on the **political will** to enact such reforms. While there is growing support for UBI, particularly in **tech circles**, **progressive** communities, and among certain economists, significant resistance remains from **conservative** and **neoliberal** factions. The main challenge lies in overcoming **political inertia**, convincing skeptical voters, and building coalitions across political lines.

But the increasing **political feasibility** of UBI can't be ignored. The **global trend** of rising inequality and instability is pushing more governments to explore UBI-like policies. Countries like **Finland**, **Spain**, **Canada**, and **India** have run **UBI pilot programs** that offer valuable data and insights into the potential of cash transfers. These experiments may prove critical in shifting the broader political and cultural perceptions of UBI from a distant dream to a concrete policy goal.

In essence, whether UBI will become inevitable depends on whether the global political will and economic realities align to demand a new way of thinking about income distribution and social support.

Lessons from History and Modern Experiments

The Failures and Successes of the Past

History provides us with valuable lessons about the potential of universal income schemes. While UBI has never been fully implemented on a national scale, there are several notable **historical experiments** that have shaped the current debate.

One such example is the **Alaska Permanent Fund**, a long-running program that provides every resident with an annual cash dividend funded by the state's oil revenues. While not a full UBI, it has proven that **universal cash payments** can have **positive effects** on individuals and communities. Alaska's experiment has demonstrated that when people are given a financial buffer, they are more likely to invest in their education, healthcare, and personal development, rather than becoming dependent or wasteful.

Similarly, the **Finnish UBI trial**, which began in 2017, provided a glimpse into the practical challenges and benefits of UBI. While the trial showed that UBI recipients experienced **improved mental well-being** and **reduced stress**, it did not show conclusive evidence of improved employment outcomes. Nevertheless, Finland's trial highlighted the **value of UBI in fostering social and psychological stability**, even if its impact on job creation was not immediate.

Additionally, in the U.S., **stocked pilot programs** like the **Oakland and Stockton UBI trials** have received wide acclaim for showing that **direct cash transfers** can improve recipients' **mental health**, **financial security**, and **employment outcomes**. These real-world applications demonstrate that UBI is more than an abstract theory—it has tangible, positive effects on people's lives, particularly for those facing economic hardship.

What Have We Learned?

Modern experiments have underscored several key lessons for the future of UBI:

1 **People don't become lazy or unproductive** with cash assistance. Evidence shows that **financial security** encourages recipients to pursue education, create businesses, and engage in community activities.

2 **UBI reduces stress and improves mental health** helping individuals and families feel more empowered and able to thrive.

3 **Conditionality is not always necessary** People can make informed, responsible decisions about their finances without strict requirements or supervision.

4 **Universal programs are more efficient** and easier to administer than complex, targeted welfare systems.

These findings suggest that UBI, if implemented properly, could address some of the key flaws in existing social safety nets, making it a more equitable, efficient, and effective means of supporting individuals in an increasingly uncertain world.

The Next Steps in the Global UBI Movement

Scaling Up Pilot Programs and Gathering Data

One of the most crucial next steps in the global UBI movement is the continued **expansion of pilot programs** and data collection. More trials are needed to understand the **long-term effects** of UBI and to refine the implementation model. These trials should include diverse geographical regions, socio-economic groups, and age demographics to gather comprehensive data on UBI's impacts.

Furthermore, these programs should aim to address **policy questions** such as the **source of funding**, **income thresholds**, and **administrative efficiency**. What works in one country or region may not be directly applicable to others, so it's vital to test different models and gather **evidence-based insights**.

Building Political and Public Support

For UBI to move from experimental phases to national policy, **political support** will be crucial. This requires engaging with various **political ideologies**, from **libertarians** advocating for a streamlined government to **progressives** seeking more robust social safety nets. UBI must be positioned as a **common-sense solution** that transcends partisan divides and appeals to a broad range of constituencies.

Building **public support** is also essential. The key to this lies in **education**—educating the public about the **benefits** of UBI, the **evidence** from pilot programs, and how UBI can address systemic issues like **inequality**, **poverty**, and **job displacement** due to automation. Public trust in UBI will be critical to overcoming resistance from skeptical voters and powerful interest groups.

Global Cooperation and Advocacy

The success of UBI will require **international cooperation**. As automation and economic inequality are **global issues**, addressing them may require coordinated efforts among countries. Through global alliances and **advocacy networks**, UBI supporters can push for policy changes that promote social justice and economic sustainability across borders.

Advocacy groups, **think tanks**, and **grassroots organizations** will play a pivotal role in pushing UBI to the forefront of political debates, advocating for both **national and international** UBI initiatives. The global movement for

UBI is gaining momentum, but it will need continuous advocacy to secure its future.

Conclusion: A New Economic Era

The future of **Universal Basic Income** rests on **the political will** to embrace it as an integral part of the economic and social fabric. While UBI may not be inevitable just yet, its **momentum** is undeniable. As more data comes in from real-world experiments, the **idea** of UBI is growing stronger, and its implementation appears more feasible than ever.

The lessons from history and modern-day trials give us a blueprint for the **success** of UBI: **efficiency**, **empowerment**, and **equity** are at the heart of its potential. By moving forward with **pilot programs**, **scaling up** successful models, and engaging in **global advocacy**, we can ensure that UBI is not just a **vision of the future**, but a **reality** that can help create a fairer, more resilient society.

The next steps are clear: **continued experimentation**, **public education**, and **political advocacy** will be the driving forces behind UBI's path to success. And while the road ahead may be challenging, one thing is certain—the idea of **Universal Basic Income** is poised to redefine the future of work, security, and justice for all.

ABOUT THE AUTHOR

Dan Paul writes books on progressive radical and sustainable alternatives to the dominant codes. With decades of experience in the economic oppression of the United States, he is uncomfortably aware of the consequences of not having enough money to live and motivated to help fellow citizens avoid the oppressive codes of the dominant society.

ALSO BY DAN PAUL

Philosophy of Action Design and Multiplicity by Dan Paul

Book 1 Auto FreeDesign

Book 2 Workers Health Handbook

Book 3 Save Your Life Prevent Hospital Use

Book 4 Coop OwnersHandbook

Book 5 Eye on AI Meeting NeedsSustainably

Book 6 Travels on the NomadicTerrain

Book 7 Tales of the UrbanShaman

Book 8 Housing in the Danger Zone

Book 9 CoronaTime

Book 10 Philosophy of Design, Action and Multiplicity

Landlords and Tenants Against Eviction

Auto Free USA

AI Frankstein Concise, Critical, Common Sense Artificial Intelligence

Forever Flowers Requiem in the Land of Milk and Honey

Websites

https://viaradmedia.org

https://autofreedesign.com

http://workershealthhandbook.com

http://sylphu.com

Social Media

https://www.facebook.com/profile.php?id=61555599616489

https://twitter.com/jonblu

https://www.instagram.com/jonblu61/

Made in the USA
Monee, IL
09 November 2026

67380381R00062